ASKING THE RIGHT QUESTIONS

ASKING THE RIGHT QUESTIONS

Dmitry Eremenko

ASKING THE RIGHT QUESTIONS

Copyright © 2025 by Dmitry Eremenko
Published by Black Pawn Press
First Edition
Print ISBN: 978-1-949802-55-9
Ebook ISBN: 978-1-949802-56-6
Printed in the United States of America

No part of this book may be used or reproduced, stored in a retrieval system, or transmitted in any form or by any means, electronic, mechanical, photocopying, recording, or otherwise, without the prior written permission of the author except in the case of brief quotations embodied in critical articles or reviews.

ASKING THE RIGHT QUESTIONS

TABLE OF CONTENTS

From the Author	vii
1. Strength of Materials vs. The Russian Federation	1
2. Clear Rules	9
3. That's How It Should Be	24
4. Two Simple Options	71
5. The Price of Compromise	32
6. "Lost Boys"	39
7. Mimics	48
8. A Taste for Blood	56
9. Big Body	64
10. The Big Breakthrough	71
11. Change for Change's Sake	80
12. All Kidding Aside	89
13. In Search of Support	98
14. Ready-made Answers (or, "Among Civilized People")	107
15. So-So Prospects	117
16. A Loss of Meaning	125
17. Ghastly Tales	133
18. Get Rid of Crutches	142
19. Last Step s	149
About the Author	154

Dmitry Eremenko

ASKING THE RIGHT QUESTIONS

FROM THE AUTHOR

Do you know such a feeling, where everything that you had previously taken for granted is now coming apart at the seams, and you have been nullified like a character in a computer game? No, worse—because you can reload a game to start again from an earlier save, but no one will give you back the years you've lost.

If this situation sounds familiar to you, then read on.

I was born in the mid-'60s in the Soviet Union. From the time we were children, my peers and I were told that we were part of the greatest System in the world. It would let us know what was "good" and what was "bad," and things would turn out better for us with our System than with any other if we did everything exactly as we were told.

I think that somewhere in the hostile West, my foreign peers were indoctrinated into something quite similar.

At first, the System looks like a set of rules that people establish and explain the need for them to you. They are also watching how you follow these rules, reward you for obedience, and punish you for violations. On the other hand, the System gives you protection and the pride of being a part of something much larger than you can understand. As far as our hopes for a safe and better life linked with the System, we have to defend it from all encroachments.

What was better for an ambitious Soviet teenager in the early '80s than becoming "2 in 1"—an army officer and computer engineer in the space program at the same time? So, I graduated from the academy with an award and became a part of great projects, full of hopes and highest expectations.

I believed and did my best to be a team player. But as I gained more knowledge and experience, explanations about the System—which was supposed to be the best around the world—became more difficult to swallow. Especially because I used to work on computers of second generations like the M-220 or BESM-6, which were more than twenty years old and based on transistors. These machines had big peripheral data storage devices. For example, for 200 kilobytes we used a steel cylinder weighing 150 kilograms. We had to clean all of it regularly with 96-percent pure alcohol. This liquid evaporated so quickly that we used it for a better purpose: for fighting stress. Such important details helped to drown out any doubts—until we sobered up.

My confidence that we were outpacing everyone everywhere collapsed when I saw an IBM PC for the first time. This toy was inferior to the domestic monsters in one respect: there was no need to use the same amount of alcohol for maintenance.

Step by step, we realized the distance between the System's promises and reality. In the end, the Soviet Union's collapse was provoked by a coup d'état in August of 1991, when the conservative elite tried to stop President Gorbachev's attempts to modify and save the failing state. It was the first time I got such clear cognitive dissonance: I had to obey some person with all attributes of ultimate power, telling me from TV about the resurrection of the great state, safety, and wellness for everyone—but I did not believe him at all. It was an even more interesting feeling, as I was an army officer and had to be ready to take my gun and follow instructions if I was ordered to. If I hesitated or argued, it would be considered a crime.

The next day I wrote a letter of resignation.

By the way, the winners of August of 1991, with no less enthusiasm, were shooting each other in October of 1993, fighting the next round of power struggle.

It was clear what the System wanted from me and what was in store for me a day ago—but all of that was ruined in the course of a week. It was some comfort that I had been traveling light because I had no family and no obligations. I did not have anything that wouldn't fit in one suitcase. It was not all bad. What's more, there was still some hope of getting some compensation for what was promised to me for eleven years of service: the possibility of getting a small apartment to live in.

To check on this possibility, I went to the military commissariat. In line in front of me, a sturdy captain of the second rank howled softly in impotence. It was the usual situation of those times—he came in the hope that the System would find a place for him from another side of the country, which was divided into parts by the former top bureaucracy. The clerk had just told him from the window: The System on which this officer used to rely now no longer knew where his family would sleep in a few days, nor how he would feed them. Then all that remained was to throw away my expectations of the System's gratitude and support to leave them on the battered floor of the military commissariat, along with my place in line.

A little later, some smart people on TV explained what the better and more liberal version of the System looked like: free market, democracy, freedom, and so on. Now everything would be fine. And again, they made some mistakes during the implementation of these good initiatives.

It's quite usual to ask ourselves at the time of big changes: *What must I do to keep everything from resetting to zero again, to ensure that the day or year that I have lived is worth something when the next big change begins?*

There is one upside in failed attempts to understand something: If we can avoid focusing on the emotions and the pain, then we can still learn from them. After all, unless you are Robinson Crusoe or a hermit, each of us faces the same task every day: We need to build relationships with other people.

I do not pretend to challenge anybody's correctness. Instead, I am just looking at these issues, in terms of practice, from their point of view. I will use my own cases mostly, but I am pretty sure that you can discover similar logic wherever you live—just take a closer look without prejudice. Basically, all of us are humans first, and I suppose that such attributes as language or citizenship do not make so much sense.

I propose that we consider everything we might call a System as something whole: common tasks, the rules that help in the completion of these tasks, and the people who formulate these rules and direct their implementation. It takes place in any country at any time since the first tribes of people arrived. We speak now about the System as some universal concept. The System sets the algorithms of our interactions and helps us understand what should and should not be done. Ideally, these algorithms are comprehensible and free of contradictions, leading to a simple choice between "yes" or "no" that can help us achieve the desired result. Otherwise, why would we need a whole System with its own rules, bosses, and directors?

For starters, there are two conditions for moving ahead.

Firstly, it's better to avoid getting personal. Seeking out and punishing the guilty is usually the quickest and easiest answer, but does not often equal the solution to the problem. Any professional manager has to check two possible reasons for failure: the wrong executive in charge, or mistakes in a task setting. The error might lie in the formulation of the problem itself or incorrectly defined conditions. So long as those are not set correctly, we will continue to accuse and punish, diversifying this process as best we can, while remaining along a well-trodden path that at times leads somewhere to the side of our common goal.

In short, if you're looking for an excuse to get your knickers in a twist, this book is not for you.

Secondly, I suggest that behind all definitions and generalizations, behind the loudest and the smartest words, there is always a person. This person, like each of us, imbues what is said with their own meaning—and this meaning does not always dovetail with all participants in the conversation. If we can begin with the simplest things that we can understand and represent identically (at least, in the broad strokes), then our discussion will not remain just another empty exercise in rhetoric (and will, in fact, lead us somewhere). Otherwise, everyone will just end up proving their own subjective truth to themselves and it will all come to nothing. Even worse, people can say the exact same words in the exact same language and come to completely different conclusions.

The rules by which our System operates are also recorded in

specifically chosen words. We must avoid variant readings as much as possible if we want the System to function.

Have doubts? Then here's a story about the issues of mutual understanding that led me to change radically my attitude to my own words—and those of others—as to written and unwritten codes. It's also an example of a distorted System that creates a kind of "twilight zone" whose inhabitants have their own ideas about what are normal and familiar rules, worked out in unpredictable ways.

As far as my work in a space program, the great Soviet Union was finished in such a funny way, I tried to adapt to the changing environment and find a new place for myself. My honors diploma and talent for keeping ancient computers alive soon turned out to be unnecessary—I had to try my hand at something else. As many people around me had no idea, I just followed a chain of casual acquaintances. The situation developed in such a way that the sale of non-ferrous metals for export showed the most alluring business prospects.

After a few successful deals, my friend and I, accompanied by our new partners, flew to Norilsk, an industrial city located in northern Siberia, to conclude a promising contract. There we were met by local "relations specialists" from the *Zavenyagin* plant (after privatization, it would become the basis for *Norilsk Nickel Group*).

To tell the truth, I had imagined my future business partners a little differently. Although goodness knows what they should look like, these Norilsk businessmen! In all that happy time of change, my capacity for surprise was the fastest to atrophy. One of them was clearly a man with a checkered past. That was evident in his almost eyebrowless face, crisscrossed by traces of countless cuts and, when I looked closely at his right hand, any further doubts left me. This hand had obviously thrown a lot of hard punches, not having bothered to protect itself with bandages or gloves, so its own bones had broken. This man, hereinafter referred to as Righty, stayed mostly silent, listening to a conversation full of meaningful and sometimes incomprehensible allusions. For the most part, I allowed them to pass me by, trying not to demonstrate my ignorance.

Around the third day of negotiations, Righty finally intervened and asked us the main question:

"Alright, this is all crap. When will you be repaying your debt?"

"What do you mean?"

"*Half a million…bucks…*"

He spat this incredible amount out with formless lips, and reality changed in the same second. The odd allusions they'd made, to which I had assigned no importance—every carelessly spoken word—all gathered together in an unexpected logical construction. From it followed that we already had obligations and had flown to Norilsk to address them.

Step by step, one simple step after another, I stubbornly tried to reassemble my version of reality. It was not a simple task, especially since everything that had been said over the past few days had begun to take on a completely different and sinister meaning. I had a feeling that I did not understand my own words.

That deal had been a trap from the very start; the "profitable proposal" and invitation to Norilsk was the bait. Our would-be business partners had become dependent on Righty's group before we met. Unlucky businessmen tried to solve their own problem by ensnaring the next potential victims, giving Righty a formal reason for an attack. Nevertheless, they had failed to defend their version of a story about "half a million bucks," which was initially a fake. Now they were "muskrats," a colloquialism in Russia for used-up human material.[1]

Clarifying terminology was also not the best idea. The "hosts" were not particularly patient and quickly moved on to demonstrative arguments. Righty began beating our former potential partners "into meat." What do I mean by "into meat"? The diet of the hotel's inhabitants consisted primarily of grilled chicken from the local buffet, slathered eternally with ketchup. We would all meet there and suspiciously recognize in our neighbors the very same "fortune hunters." Evidently, this was

---

[1] Why "muskrat"? Apparently, it was because of the uniform by which a freshly arrived entrepreneur could be identified in the winter Norilsk (-40 °C) of the early '90s: the invariable "cashmere" coat made of a material similar to wool, the ushanka hat with earflaps of mink, raccoon, or beaver.

why, the next day, the maid in our suite started cursing the idiots who had splashed sauce all over the walls... until she realized that it wasn't splashes of ketchup and rushed out of the room.

The "locals" still had their own "underworld code." It might seem strange, but, in accordance with these rules, it was necessary that we somehow accept their logic. We had only to agree and confirm just a small part of imposed obligations and, perhaps, it would all work out. This, however, was made more difficult by the shapeless pile of rags and flesh against the wall of the hotel room, splashed with something red—the carcass of the "muskrat," awaiting the next "round of negotiations." Any "maybe," well, sure," half-agreement, or uncertain step, and you could end up there.

Nevertheless, they were unable to shove us into their scenario within several days. Now we were offered the option of concluding the deal for the purchase of metal anyway, with the support of local "specialists"—this time, however, with the "right seller." The choice was small—or, rather, practically nonexistent, since there were only two ways out of the city: either through the port on the Yenisei River or the airport. In either case, you would have to drive several tens of kilometers along a road that was periodically blocked due to snowstorms. Furthermore, there was nothing to be done without a passport, and these had been taken away from us as soon as we had been declared debtors.

When in an unfamiliar subarctic city in the middle of a harsh frost, and other escape routes do not spring quickly to mind, the only option that remains is to agree with the new proposal.

I arrived at the meeting to conclude the promised deal and gave Righty's name as a kind of strange password. They didn't argue with me; they just asked that I drop back in after a couple of hours. So, I came back a bit later. This time, two new characters in suits met me and flashed IDs that indicated that they were state security officers. The illusion that this was an opportunity for salvation sparked in my brain. It was good that it only sparked, because the hope of returning to my typical reality proved to be just another facet of the world behind the Looking Glass.

Once again, I was being slotted into another logical structure that only a few days ago I would have considered incredible. In full, perfect Russian, without unfamiliar slang, official terms sprinkled throughout for flavor, they painted me a picture of their own version of the proceedings. It turned out that we had encroached on the territory where another predator had already been feeding. He jealously guarded his subordinates, whom we were trying to force to conclude an agreement, threatening and acting in the name of criminal authority. In fact, according to my interlocutors, I myself was an accomplice or a member of a criminal gang. The easiest way out was to "enter into cooperation" with them—for which, in return, they would not devour me. Maybe they wouldn't devour me. I was forced to answer with grudging and unequivocal phrases, knowing full well that my own judgment and sentence might turn out to be composed of my own words. And so on and so forth, until they let me go with the promise that I would "think long and hard and make the right choice."

Now I had to go back to the hotel and share with Righty and his group this new turn of events. From their emotional reaction, it was difficult to tell what they wanted now (and, even more difficult, what they planned to do with us next). Several more meetings with both sides followed, and for several endless hours I would speak in short, choppy sentences, hardly recognizing my own simple and familiar language. I had to feel them out, almost blindly, guessing what my own and others' words now meant and how their logic functioned—the logic according to which they had built a plan for my near future. It's funny that, in both instances, it was necessary to repeat the same phrases, avoiding complex constructions as much as possible. Drawing them out under pressure, trying to give neither predator an excuse for brute force, and hoping that, sooner or later, they would lose interest.

In the end, it seemed as though we managed to find the right words that helped to avoid pitfalls, and this adventure concluded almost without consequence.

Half a year later, there occurred another conversation with Righty. He told me about how a promising, underage boxer, who, following some unwritten rules of his own, had accidentally killed a man with his bare hands for the first time. How he had spent eighteen of his thirty-six years in prison, not the least because he

ASKING THE RIGHT QUESTIONS

continued to rigorously observe his own laws. How he had been released and tried to familiarize himself outside a cage: *"I don't understand, I don't understand anything here..."*

These were some of the few human words I heard from him.

The code of "twilight zone" divided everyone into predators and prey and explained why the predator was always in the right. Following this logic, he was far from the smallest predator, and I originally was prey. To put his right hand into action, however, he was lacking a bit in confidence. Another player, whom I initially perceived as a protector, turned out to be a predator as well. I knew one thing for certain: Both of them had manipulated me by written and unwritten codes, but the true meaning was my place in a food chain. I had no clear understanding, just a strong feeling that my agreement or acceptance of their versions of truth would make my next day even worse than what was happening in the here and now. It helped me a lot in standing on my shaky legs.

Yes, I'm talking about words—so familiar to us that we hardly even think about how our interlocutor understands them, supposing that everything is clear. When we are called upon to specify their meaning, these words can suddenly become terribly heavy, slippery, spiky, and inappropriate. Imperceptibly, in pieces and separate details, another person, following their own understanding of the rules, can conjure your nightmare out of these words.

That's why we'll start our conversation about the System with something simple and comprehensible. In the next chapter, I'll speak about my research about the erosion of objective knowledge that has made me doubt that there is any logic to the System and led me to astonishing discoveries about our national mentality.

Dmitry Eremenko

ASKING THE RIGHT QUESTIONS

~ CHAPTER ONE ~
# STRENGTH OF MATERIALS VS. THE RUSSIAN FEDERATION

It's best to start with the solution of an understandable issue. That way, we can see how the System handles it, conjuring the incomprehensible from the perfectly understandable. It is furthermore worth thinking about what kind of result we'll get with the help of such a System.

From that story about Norilsk, it's not difficult to guess that working with metals didn't turn out great for me. Ten years later, having learned a little, I started working as a freelancer in business plan development. These feasibility studies were focused on the transfer of modern technologies of polymer processing to Russia and usually involved large sums of money, but the work paid very little. It soon became clear that nothing would change if at least one of these fascinating ideas was not verified through practice. To do this, we had to start small: selling at least a little of the product that we were planning to offer by putting some of it into production. Those who were paying me for business plans didn't appreciate this. It was one thing, after all, to earn millions on Excel spreadsheets and to negotiate impressive commissions, but quite another to work with fickle customers, modest amounts of money, and a wealth of minute details.

On top of that, the very first project I managed to bring to fruition, a city sewer repair program, didn't go at all as planned. In the presentations I gave the clients my data, everything looked very simple and convincing. It was just that the people who were supposed to be doing this work at a depth of twenty meters below the ground in an old two-meter concrete pipe were not privy to these presentations. They were going to have to reproduce everything shown in the pictures while almost waist-deep in the current flowing through this same sewer.

Questions arose of their own accord and the originator of this proposal—that is, me—was encouraged to figure it all out. A refusal to do so would reduce my chances of further success to zero. A university course in economics didn't help very much here, but luckily my years of military service taught me to approach most things without trepidation or hesitation. What had to be done, had to be done.

Yeah... In the presentations, everything was much simpler. There was no stench, even though it didn't take long to get used to. There was also no surefire way to find out when people would be coming home and turning on the taps to wash, do laundry, and cook. In reality, the sewage level would rise quickly and knock workers off their feet. And the worst thing for anyone working in the sewer pipe was the unexpected downpour. In those instances, it was imperative to run with all possible speed to the nearest ladder to keep from being washed away.

Million-dollar contracts, work at an international holding, and a nice company car would come later, but, for the moment, I was sitting on a tile floor under a sink and feeling very, very bad. After a day spent "downstairs," I was experiencing all the symptoms of severe poisoning and attempting to understand the reaction of my body, offended by such treatment.

Rhetorical questions were fulfilling the role of an additional toxin: What was I not understanding, what lessons did I miss or lectures did I skip for no good reason? What had I done wrong and who was to blame for the fact that in my forties I had not found anything better to do than wallow about in somebody else's shit?

In the end, everything worked out and a year later the European company that offered up the production technology agreed it was necessary to establish a subsidiary company consisting of one person (me) and a rented desk in someone else's office. There were no budgets or investments as such, but I was assigned a supervisor from German North Rhine-Westphalia. It was useless trying to throw pity parties or explain to him all the difficulties that came along with the application of the new product. He clarified the situation once and for all by saying something like:

"We're paying you money. If everything were that simple, why would we have contracted you?" After that, I tried not to tell him about any more difficulties.

One of these specific problems was the need to obtain all the required regulatory approvals and clearances from our System. The "specially trained people" didn't really explain anything. They rolled their eyes a lot, pointed to someplace up above, and offered to arrange everything "as it should be." For an additional fee, of course. But I wasn't given any money for this, so I had to think of something else.

For my supervisor, the intricacies of local regulation turned out to be an unexpectedly simple issue. Step by step, he reduced all conversations to a matter of purely technical problems to be solved with the assistance of an elementary school physics course. All I had to do was remember what grade I was in when I took said knowledge. He also made me wonder why so many people, instead of doing a few mathematical equations, speak and write so many unnecessary buzzwords of bureaucratic casuistry.

Since our products were, in particular, used for the construction and repair of sewers, we had to demonstrate the reliability of the structures that could be built from our materials. This task could be divided into three fundamental parts. First: Determine the load rating and working conditions. Second: Find material of the right size and shape, durable enough to support these loads for as long as we need. Third: Make certain that the characteristics of the selected option are not spun out of thin air but are rather confirmed via the necessary tests and calculations.

I had to review Soviet textbooks and find that everything there was the same. If there was a difference with the European approach, it was in the details. In the European formulation, the main requirements of the task were determined, a methodology for their implementation was proposed, and the choice of the final version was left (along with the responsibility) to the one fulfilling the task. In a planned economy like the Soviet Union, that variety of calculated situations and the need to think independently were typically replaced by a choice between a couple of permissible options. Taking these newly learned lessons as a basis, I began to decipher the claims in the documents and procedures, trying to puzzle out their logic.

But if everything were that simple…

The unbelievable complexity of our approach to technical issues, taking the place of simple "yes/no" algorithms, soon became apparent. It turned out that, in local conditions, calculation was more of a tribute to a half-forgotten tradition than a necessity. In practice, it was better to find something appropriate, already approved and demonstrated to be effective, in order to copy it and pass all the clearances along a well-trodden track. The easiest way was to compose the document using well-known templates and collect as many signatures and seals on the title page as possible. If you propose using one's brain to remember what we were all taught, then you've already lost. This habit, inherited from the planned economy, of relying not on calculations but on documents hasn't gone anywhere. When I tried to substantiate the advantages of our solutions using calculations and evidence, I was invariably asked for some sort of certificate that my interlocutors often could not describe or explain where to get the necessary permission. The best evidence was considered to be a resolution from the boss, shutting down all questions along with the ability to think. Here I'll quote a participant in one of these meetings, practically verbatim: "In our country, strength of materials doesn't hold sway—the laws of the Russian Federation do," and "We don't need theories, we work according to approved regulations."

After determining that turning to physics textbooks was not going to be helpful, I decided to seek answers in those previously mentioned laws of the Russian Federation. The correct formulation of the problem was finally found—in the fundamental federal law, "Technical Regulations on the Safety of Buildings and Structures," no less. Hooray! There it was written that the safety of structures had still to be ensured by calculations. But right there in the text, someone very crafty (or very stupid) proposed that the same issue could be solved "in other ways," namely, by establishing reliability via reference to the requirements of standards included in the roster for mandatory adoption by the Prime Minister. That is, anything not included on such a roster had nothing to do with our task of establishing reliability. Although, in that same roster, the standard that describes in detail the need for calculations and evidence is the

ASKING THE RIGHT QUESTIONS

first point. But to see this, you have to dive into the content that comes after the headings.

If we take the same product with which we solve the same problem, then the requirements and the procedure for their fulfillment logically ought to be the same for everyone. The contents of the technical specifications for one product produced by various manufacturers should not be fundamentally different from one to another. Fat chance. Here we can have several standards governing one product simultaneously, and they will only differ in the degree of their disregard for the laws of physics and common sense. Each manufacturer can compose and approve their own technical specifications, discarding anything inconvenient for them, including the most important: evidence without which the solution to the reliability problem loses all meaning.

We've severed the logical connection between the norms document and the technical task imbuing the document with meaning. Now, you can write anything down on paper so long as you follow the registration rules and complete all the bureaucratic rituals. The product's service life does not need to be demonstrated through experimentation and the destruction of the required number of samples, limiting yourself by rejecting the cheapest low-quality raw materials. So, you can just write "service life of 100 years" on your document and the System has accepted it as proof.

I had to make sure that this wasn't a mistake or a separate failure in the System, and then try to fix something. To do this, I started turning to the people who controlled the implementation of that very federal law and should, in theory, have understood issues of reliability and safety. I began with construction committees, state experts, and even sectoral federal ministries. None of them wanted to dwell on that line in the federal law where it was stated that calculations were required. Everyone confidently skipped that part and moved on to the references to standards from the approved roster. So, my counterparts redirected me to the other one several times, and then they sent me together...over the rainbow. There, where the last echelon of authority dwelt, the Prime Minister. This appealed to the very top worked, but the question was nonetheless passed back to the relevant technical committee to work it out.

At a session of the technical committee, I heard a dozen words that people usually say when they're lying a little, and then a hundred more that help them not to admit it. The discussion again turned to how, in our case, we should demonstrate the reliability of our product in repairing urban sewage systems.

My initial assumption was that in terms of physiology and chemical composition, the byproducts of Russians' vital activities could not be fundamentally different from what the rest of humanity produces. Why, then, could we not perform the required tests and simulate operating conditions like they do in the rest of the world using a sulfuric acid environment? After all, the "substance" we all produce smells the same—hydrogen sulfide. And then...

Bam! The truth went splat onto the table. It was a patriotic postulate that the European approach to the chemical composition of feces did not apply to Russian conditions for a variety of reasons, the first of which was because of a... *difference in mentality.*

The drum roll subsided, the face of the speaker taking on an expression that corresponded well to the moment: his cheeks puffing out, his eyes upwards. The rest, appreciating the depth and weight of the statement, began to exchange glances and nod in agreement.

I quickly recovered from my concussion and tried to clarify. The image was funny, at first. Guys, if your national mentality has such a drastic effect on your bowel movements, then there's probably something wrong with it...

My flippant reaction inspired a strange metamorphosis among the members of this learned assembly. Their eyes turned inside their heads and started to resemble buttons. Practically in unison, they began to blow hot air at each other, using language for the record to describe my unseemly and unpatriotic behavior, completely inappropriate when discussing matters of such importance. It got uncomfortable, because it all looked like a scene from a movie where people are being mind-controlled. Was I the one in the wrong or was there something wrong with them? *Maybe I ought to try thinking in unison with others to achieve general enlightenment and not cling so tightly to my own.*

The result of this gathering was a summary protocol, or a

depressing exercise spread across six pages of buzzwords that made no sense. It still had to be worked over in a meeting at the federal agency responsible for standardization, where there were fewer participants and such deep thoughts neither fell onto the table with such deafening volume nor were received with such reverence. In the end, they promised to set everything in working order and to "bring it into balance" over the next two or so years (as of 2023, seven years have passed without the slightest change).

I asked: What about the fact that confusing standards that we discussed before remain valid and not entirely reliable products currently being used in construction? In response, they sent me to the Ministry of Construction.

In reply to an appeal to the Ministry of Construction, I received yet another Truth. The safety of buildings and structures has nothing to do with the technical specifications of the material from which they are built. This was because the standards that govern these materials are not located on the same roster personally approved by the Prime Minister. In short, this roster did not happen to include a physics textbook, and the Prime Minister didn't feel the need to read one and make calculations.

One final control request to "get closure," again through the very top, the office of the Prime Minister (as the ministries had ceased to answer me by any other avenue): "The idea that the properties of the building materials have nothing to do with the reliability of the things we're constructing—are you serious or is the clerk who wrote this just talking nonsense?" Answer: "Yes, completely serious, and please refrain from contacting us again, we will no longer be responding to your frivolous appeals."

Our quest led to a disappointing conclusion. Formulas for problem-solving, though familiar to us even from high school, are not the norm but the exception. In practice, it's enough to slap together a suitable justification from tired formulations and push the real solution into the background. Then wait and see what happens—although the obvious way to solve the problem is not to try to cheat the laws of physics. They'll definitely mete out a punishment for error or an attempt to circumvent them. The laws of nature will do it, and they'll manage without adhering to approved regulations. After all, that's physics for you...

This one is just a sample—we'll find a clear and solid foothold of knowledge that enables us to see how our System works and how it handles the solutions to its problems. I'm certain that, in any field, one can start with something evident to anyone who's studied the issue in order to arrive at a similar conclusion.

All of us are economic subjects and have our own tasks to get all we need in return. The more complex the task, the more difficult it is to find the correct formulation of the question that leads to an unambiguous answer of "yes" or "no." The System ought to help us find methods of management and interaction. But in this described case, we build our own methods of cooperation, making common mistakes and establishing, with the help of our System, new ways to lose where we ought to have earned. The farther we go, the bigger the likelihood that one of us will decide not to put in any effort, instead following the path of least resistance and accepting a ready-made answer from the System, succumbing to the principle of "That's how it should be" in place of logic and common sense.

Let's overlook this accusatory sentiment and just deal with the mechanics of the processes we've set into motion with such a substitution.

~ CHAPTER TWO ~
CLEAR RULES

Let's start by talking about the System and its algorithms that describe people's interactions with rules that work in the realm of the explicable; those that, if desired, can be supported with exhaustive evidence.

The question of integrity or, rather, the security of any economic transaction in which at least two people are participating, should begin with a clear and comprehensible definition of what will constitute a true or positive result for both parties. And the opposite—they must define minimum requirements, the violation of which will lead to an unambiguous and firm "no."

Now I'll sketch a general schema using well-known examples: How were the tools for solving these problems of economic transactions found and how did they serve at the end as the basis for universal rules operating in the conditions of globalization?

In the economy of an ancient or medieval market, people made simple and understandable arrangements. There was no particular need to write down general rules because usually they spoke about something well-known to both sides. It was necessary to make sure that both the buyer and seller viewed the subject of the transaction in the same way, at least in basic terms. A reference sample or benchmark was used as the most accessible tool for arbitration. For example, at a seasonal wool fair, one parcel with the "correct" volume and quality would be selected for this purpose. Anything no worse in quality or less in quantity than the sample was traded, and all that remained was to determine the price. If someone tried to sneak in below-standard goods, then this seller was dealt with using all the bluntness characteristic of the Middle Ages.

When it came to complex items such as a big ship or building, these were sorted out individually, relying on experience, reputation, and carefully guarded professional secrets that in actuality could turn out to be false. Mathematical instruments for measuring and describing the subject of the transaction had as of yet not been invented, and some of them remained for centuries beneath the rubble of Hellenistic culture, destroyed by religious dogmatics. Metric systems had not yet been adopted and there were practically no calculations capable of arriving at and subsequently reproducing a successful solution of a challenging task. Only their authors could transfer these solutions from object to object, using their own experience of trial and error.

A big progress was achieved through the implementation of mathematical modeling. The era of geographic discoveries dawned in the 16th century. The primary arena for technological competition was the sea, and the decisive argument was for the mass construction of armed ships that helped to put these discoveries to use.

No one could confidently calculate the displacement of a future ship. The empty hull would be built on the shore, and it remained to determine at what height cannon ports should be cut through and the decks laid. The shell with its spacers would be lowered into the water, loaded with ballast, and then, already on the water, the rest of the ship would be completed almost in its entirety. The key to success was having faith in the canonical proportions worked out by experience and the knowledge passed from master to master. If the shipbuilder didn't have the authority and self-confidence to measure up against an important customer, the price of compliance would be hundreds of human lives and the loss of impressive investments. This is what happened to the *Vasa*, a ship in whose construction the "Lion of the North," Gustav II Adolph, interfered with too enthusiastically. The warrior-king wanted lots of cannons, and he got them. The ship set off on its maiden voyage, fired a salute from these cannons, lost its steadiness, and sank to the depths before the eyes of the public. Luckily, we now have the opportunity in Stockholm to witness this wonder made from the trunks of 10,000 oaks, raised to the surface four centuries later.

Notable progress occurred in the 17th century. Archimedes came to mind very opportunely with his bathing caused Eureka moment, Johann Kepler became interested in the volume of a wine barrel and found integrals in it, while Simon Stevin depicted resultant forces and introduced decimal fractions. Gradually, dogmas blurred and instruments appeared that were brought together to solve a practical problem by the Englishman Sir Anthony Deane. This hotshot was not yet thirty when he calculated a ship's displacement using drawings, determined the position of the decks, and cut the broadsides of his first battleship while still on the slipway.

He gambled and won. When the hull was launched into the water, Deane, in company with Archimedes, Galileo, and Kepler, turned out to be correct. First displacement, and later the other most important characteristics of a ship no longer had to be guessed at. It now became possible to specify and calculate them.

In England, Sir Anthony's experience made it possible to launch almost-finished ships into the water, and within a few decades, all of Europe was following this example. There were, perhaps, fewer masterpieces and extraordinary specimens, but, at last, they were able to achieve the desired results in a simpler and more logical way that could be replicated. One specialist could reproduce the success of another without resorting to blind imitation by using the mathematical model developed by a colleague. Calculations became a working tool that supplanted canonical proportions and the trial-and-error method.

Two centuries passed before humanity took the next step and the fruits of progress became available to a wide range of non-specialists. In the 19th century, the proliferation of steam engines was held up by one unfortunate development: An error committed during manufacture or operation could turn the apparatus into a bomb of sizable destructive power. Many of those who would benefit from the power of steam energy had neither the time nor the desire to wade into its intricacies—and no one wanted to risk their lives. A specially trained person was needed to grapple with this issue.

The British once again turned out to be pioneers in this area, and the Germans were quick to borrow from their experience. In the second half of the 19th century, forty-three independent organizations for the inspection of steam boilers (*DÜV: DampfkesselÜberwachungsvereine*) were founded over one decade on the territory of the future Germany alone. Specialists developed sets of rules, or standards, for how to manufacture a steam engine and how to ensure it was built to said standards. The objective knowledge available to professionals was supplemented with a clear set of conditions and control procedures that had to be fully implemented to receive the final confirmation: Your device is not a bomb.

In this sort of scenario, the manufacturer understands what the lowest limit of safety is, both for them and for their competitors. They also know what awaits them should they cross that limit. Having received confirmation from the specialist that everything has been done as it should be the seller can then go to the buyer. The choice for the buyer is also clear: If you, the buyer, don't want to take a risk, ask for an independent specialist and pay to ensure your own safety. If you don't want to pay, then experiment—but only on your own, without endangering others. Otherwise, insurance companies will make that experience very, very expensive. I repeat: Nothing superfluous, only the minimal but necessary requirements whose fulfillment allows us to be certain that the product is suitable and safe.

Over time, the same rules were required for internal combustion engines, electrical installations, and so on. Today, the heirs of the steam boiler specialists—five companies with billion-dollar turnover under the shared name TÜV—are among the leaders of the global technical audit market.

The availability and mass production of complex machinery launched the Industrial Revolution, and now it is necessary to manage risk in the face of the growing scale, complexity, and speed of economic operations. As before, we need the seller and the buyer to understand what they are agreeing on while located in different parts of the globe and not knowing each other personally.

The value of the majority of industrial products depends on how long (or how many times) they can be used for their intended purpose. A comprehensive answer to this question can only be obtained by breaking the product, but then we would have nothing to sell. Instead, it's better to determine a useful resource by destroying a number of prototypes and processing the results with the help of statistics. Then, an algorithm is established through which the characteristics of the samples destroyed in the testing process are transferred to the serial product. Ultimately, we must make certain that each mass-produced product meets all mandatory requirements with a probability of at least, for example, 97.5 percent. The remaining 2.5 percent can be relegated to warranty obligations.

For a professional, a "100 percent guarantee" isn't worth a thing. This is called quality assurance with a given probability and furnishes the right to use a certain badge or sticker, or to receive a certificate. For this, evidence is provided that indicates the entire sequence of data collection and its mathematical processing has been completed in full. Then, when releasing the serial products, the seller ensures that they don't deviate from the established regulations. Buyers can hand over their money and feel secure that they haven't been deceived.

Yes, we're talking about standards or norms; that is, about the rules formulated by people armed with knowledge and understanding of the subject. A proportion of conventionality is present, but it's minimal. It's necessary so that discussions don't become endless and so that, when designing a load-bearing beam, we don't get bogged down in arguments about atomic structure. These conventions set the required level of detail demanded for the tackling of a concrete, practical task. For calculating the reliability of pipelines, we can assume that the circumference is not considered an oval until the deformation exceeds 5 percent, but if we apply the same limit to the wheel of a car, we won't get far on it.

There ought to be nothing superfluous or ambiguous. We set a lower permitted limit of quality to head off error or deception. It all boils down to a sequence of actions from which nothing can be removed or replaced. The uninitiated might perceive these procedures as a sort of ritual, but to a specialist, each link makes sense. Skipping one step, using unverified data—any deviation from the task in its correct formulation slashes our chances of producing the desired result from 97.5 percent to approximately half that. We'll call this the "Blonde Principle" (forgive the cliche), following the example of our heroine who estimated the chance of meeting a living dinosaur on the street as "50/50: Either I meet one or I don't."

Deviation from the formalized procedure that manufacturers promised to adhere to and did not is regarded as fraud. It doesn't matter whether this deviation resulted in actual damage. For example, take the scandal at the Nissan factories in Japan in 2017. The company was obliged to stop production and recall more than a million cars from the Japanese market. Later it became clear that the reason for this was that the products were assessed for quality by employees who were not properly certified, not that any flaws were discovered.

Another example is the manipulation of the Volkswagen diesel engine software, uncovered by envious Americans in 2015. An electronic device for measuring emissions levels was installed with a program that purposefully underestimated the measurement in test mode. So, the cause for billions of dollars in lawsuits and punishments for management was not the *factual damage* detected, the size of which could only be determined at the level of assumption and could be argued about for a long time. The cause of the proceedings was fraud during testing procedures.

The basis of licensing procedures for pharmaceuticals is expensive clinical trials on the same test sample, but these are substituted for lab animals and humans who have given their consent to participate. Everyone must follow the same path and move on to the next stage only after having completed the previous one in its entirety. Our hope for recovery depends on certain statistics and the assurance that no one has cheated with either the results or the procedure itself. Only in this manner can we get something new and truly useful.

In each of these examples, there is a correct formulation of the task that leads us to the only correct solution—as in a school textbook—and doesn't give rise to useless disputes. Anywhere in the world, a specialist can manage a task in the same way and, using the same variables, will arrive at the same conclusions. At the end of the day, everyone gets what they need: a stable ship, a safe steam engine, or an acceptable level of risk.

We have sketched in general terms a schema that guarantees the intensity of today's economic processes, in all their scale and complexity, and provides for effective interaction between strangers who remain unconnected in any other way. They can rely on a standard that outlines the subject of their transaction, indicate it in the contract or on the label, and are compelled to comply with its requirements. In everything else, they can believe as they like and follow their own laws.

The main thing in solving such a rather technical issue is not who is most important, but what. Rules are written and carried out by specialists and given this formulation, the problem will be solved in the same way independently of who undertakes it. In this sense, there are no bosses in the System and no need to obey anyone, no conventions or contradictions that require the mandatory participation of the state. A person with power can intervene. If there's no one else to ask, it can support and assist, but it can't offer anything fundamentally new because everything is based on objective knowledge and understanding of the task. There is just no reason to use subordination.

This schema protects participants from "threats from below" or from a little less honest colleague. It provides a foothold and direction for those who want to grow, develop, and move forward. The schema is strict and not always convenient because the least reliable link in it is the human being. It doesn't provide an answer to the most difficult question for everyone: What should I do when no one sees me? Then the rules are broken in order for someone to benefit themselves at the expense of others who can end up losing far more. The overall result depends on the ability of a group of people to identify and curb the manifestations of such an error.

In the early 2000s, Colorado Springs decided to curb spending on streetlights. Law-abiding townspeople were expected to save one million twenty-five thousand dollars, except that about five million had to be spent on restoring copper cable, which was stolen by their not-so-law-abiding neighbors while the light was turned off. No one, in the whole scope of human history, has managed to overcome this sort of failure when it comes to any endeavor in which human beings are involved. I hardly believe that anyone will succeed in the future, as far as I understand human nature.

Next, I'll speak about a more sophisticated part of the System's rules that we are not able to base on objective knowledge. Here we have no better option than to accept a concept that is suggested or dictated by certain human persons.

~ CHAPTER THREE ~
THAT'S HOW IT SHOULD BE

Ideal rules capable of answering every question can be found in approximately the same area where the ideal person lives, somewhere very far away. We follow different codes in different parts of the globe and rarely look for objective and rational explanations for them.

Together with my classmates, we used to walk on the streets in the 1970s for public holidays with banners in the most non-free country and "freedom" was written on half of these red rags. Because we were sure that is what real freedom looked like. We took it for granted as the most important part of our System, largely because some people with titles and attributes constantly repeated this actual version of the truth accompanied by boring, everyday routine and regular pompous rituals.

How often do we prove their credibility using our knowledge and simple logic? Are you sure that your source of truth wants to free you or just keep your attention playing on your emotions? Or they speak so many words because it is exactly what they do better than most of us and this job is well paid. Their argumentation is generally based on conviction rather than on objective logic but one of the greatest incentives is the fear of being like a black sheep and receiving punishment.

When it's impossible to find similar formulations for all "hows?" and "whys?", arriving at the same answers, then someone ends up determining where the border between right and wrong lies and what will happen to those who cross that border. Simultaneously, in the absence of comprehensive and satisfactory supporting evidence, these rules need to be validated somehow. The first and simplest argument was just violence, and the adoption of rules took care of the primary problem: They made it feasible to start killing each other less often. To build a sustainable System, violence in its pure form was not enough for obvious reasons—everything could change in a day with the appearance of a better-prepared challenger.

Eventually the schema became based on hereditary transmission of power, and genealogy became its most important bedrock when choosing medieval leaders. This schema was not ideal and also gave rise to periodic failure—heirs of the desired sex were not born on time, died early, or did not live up to expectations and people got such stories like the 100-year war between England and France or a lot of other dynastic conflicts.

Another method of argumentation was reliance on knowledge that was accessible and comprehensible only to a select few. These were people who usually obtained this revelation by some unique or mysterious way—through some dream or vision, achieved with meditations, hunger, contusion, or a pot with magic mushrooms. The ability to read and correctly interpret sacred texts, finding within them the necessary answers to pass them off as the "will from above" in combination with impressive rituals, also helped to fill in the gaps in the System's logic. These arguments could not be unambiguous and subjective. Disputes soon began regarding which texts could be taken as irrefutable sources of truth (that is, canonical) and which were apocrypha. It soon became clear that even the same text could be interpreted in different ways, particularly if the author was writing in a half-forgotten language and had died several centuries before. Those who preferred the incorrect texts or who were too loose in their interpretations ended up in exile or at the state declared a heretic.

Now we'll spend some time on the particularities of the System, built on the basis of such ambiguous argumentation, but determining for everyone the boundaries and definitions of what is suggested to be permitted or acceptable.

Let's start with the fact that, unlike the regulations described in the previous chapter, these rules cannot be universal for all countries or nations in any way. The rules, constructed on objective evidence, are just supplemented over time without changing their content in principle. Rules established according to the line "That's how it should be" are only functional for a certain period of time. They function only within the realm of influence of those who dictate their version of order. Both the rules themselves and the arguments in support of them can be endlessly challenged and revised depending on the circumstances.

In the 15th century, the Portuguese regained control over the southern side of Gibraltar, which had been given to the Muslims some seven centuries before and began to sail farther and farther south than anyone else, capturing the coast of Africa. They discovered new lands. And who could be asked about ownership rights for these lands besides the Pope? Who else in Europe at that time had a more impressive set of arguments? The Pope offered the Portuguese, in advance, all the unknown lands they might find to the south and east of Cape Bojador (in what is now Morocco). There was nothing interesting in the West yet—just the ocean and a few islands that had already been discovered.

But then King Ferdinand of Aragon and Queen Isabella of Castile took Granada and put an end to the last Muslim caliphate in the Iberian Peninsula. They sponsored Columbus, who had gone the farthest west of anyone and found something there similar to India. Pope Alexander VI, of the Borgia family and with Aragonian roots, ended up on the holy throne and, at the request of his countrymen, he drew a new border right through the ocean along the meridian just west of the Azores. According to the Pope, all lands discovered to the west of that line would belong to future Spaniards, while those to the east would belong to the Portuguese, and so it would be. Any violators of this arrangement would have problems with the Holy See and be subject to the consequences. No one had yet guessed about the existence of America and the Pacific Ocean, nor that there were two continents past the line. The Portuguese bargained and, just in case, moved the dividing line a little to the west, such that later they were able to find their "slice" of South America and develop it with full rights.

That's how the Pope drew the line on the map, deliberated a bit, moved his finger a hundred leagues to the west across an empty void of painted ships and Leviathans—and Brazil speaks

Portuguese to this day.

The schema that the Portuguese set up with the Spaniards immediately displeased the other European monarchs, but they had to be careful of the Holy See and the powerful Spanish fleet. A hundred years or so later, examples of disobedience on the part of Henry VIII and his daughter Elizabeth, as well as other events, forced a reevaluation of the Pope's arguments, and soon enough no one asked him about much. Other methods were found for revising established boundaries. In the 19th century, a decent chunk of North America could be bought from Napoleon at a reasonable price, or, as the United States did, one could simply brazenly put the screws to the addled heirs of the Spanish empire.

The application of rules established on the basis of "That's how it should be" will not always produce a positive result. That which had been a great success in the 16th century had already by the 17th century begun to slow and drag down. In Spain, largely due to the import of gold and silver from the New World, the Industrial Revolution was late to dawn.

Some will always have it better and some will always have it worse, and the originator of the rules that determine what is "good" and what is "bad" is the least likely to lose. Such rules require frequent refinement, as far as the level of speculation is no longer anchored to simple and comprehensible tasks, leaving a wide margin for interpretation.

However, because the bearer of the most convincing arguments cannot manage everything alone, the schema relies on a hierarchical management system. In the case of the Russian economic and political system, that hierarchy not only proved to be indispensable, but made things interesting as we got further along. For most people (myself included), you could say that our interactions with the state hierarchy were *vertical*, insofar as interactions such as these imply power and subordination, while our economic activities were *horizontal* because those interactions were based on agreements (or contracts). Those who must obey need to be convinced that the hierarchy has already thought of everything for them; therefore, all that remains is for them to accept that system as truth and believe that everything will be okay.

ASKING THE RIGHT QUESTIONS

At the same time, the interests of those who represent the System don't always coincide with those of the general public. This was a problem for the ancient Romans, and they proposed a decent solution. Two consuls were elected for one year in Roma and they got the highest military power or imperium for one year. The Republic expanded the territories under its control, maintained order and security, and achieved a stable flow of resources to the metropole. One year was not enough to fix the problem outside of the city of Roma and they were appointed proconsuls with prolongation of imperium to manage these issues within a certain territory.

Gaius Julius Caesar was appointed proconsul and given legions to clean up the mess in the northern regions for a number of years. It is known that the duration of his powers was repeatedly extended and as a result he achieved impressive successes in Gaul. He, of course, primarily put his victories to use in service of his own interests. The metropole was offended by this and called Caesar home, where he would be obliged to abide by the decisions of the Senate, then under the influence of his rival, Pompey. At the same time, Caesar was supposed to have left these local problems—along with his powers, weapons, and loyal legionnaires—across that river called the Rubicon.

One inconvenient condition was exchanged for one more suitable. Opportunely, Mark Antony, having been elected to the Tribune of the Plebs position, provoked the Senate, and provided himself with a good reason to escape and flee to Caesar for protection. Caesar then crossed the Rubicon and appeared in Rome with all of his armed, trained, and numerous arguments. Of course, he did this to save both democracy and his friend, not at all for a personal showdown with Pompey and the hostile senators. What happened to democracy afterward is well known.

Let's take from this example the concept of the Rubicon—not as a point of no return, but as a kind of border. This line separates the issues we cannot resolve without turning to "That's how it should be" and the construction of power hierarchies from those issues that can be resolved without resorting to subjugation and other ambiguous argumentation such as, for example, those described in the preceding chapter.

Step by step rituals and traditions had retreated to the

background and the power of certain people became based on the suggestion that these people knew the path to the common good for all followers better than all others. All that they need to move ahead is the only rightful concept and the stability of the entire structure relies on the persuasiveness of the correct idea or supposition around which the entire System is built. Anybody who disputes or shows any doubts, the System automatically defines him as a danger and declares him as a public enemy. Relatively harmless initial ideas formulated by some philosopher became a dogma, the last and only correct version of the holy truth, which justifies any measures of a powerful group.

But we know that the best way to prove any concept is practice. It's difficult to achieve the ends we expect when we get so carried away by our ideas that we try to prove them right at all costs. Such an experiment quickly loses all meaning in terms of obtaining a result from which some conclusions can be drawn. This is reminiscent of a science experiment in which the authors of an idea, seeking to prove its correctness, launch one lab mouse after another into a maze without altering the conditions or analyzing what is happening. The scientists in this instance are just waiting for the test subjects to start doing what they need to see. They ignore the changing environment and accept just any hint that everything is going in the right way.

What if you happened to have been born a laboratory mouse and the ultimate purpose of your entire life is to prove correct someone else's idea, proposed long before you were ever born? You're presented with conditions that elaborate on what you must do to ensure everything is okay and where you must not go to prevent things from going bad. You run towards your goal, try to stick to the task as far as you're able to understand it, and even begin to plan and guess the future. But instead of the anticipated reward, you get a shock. You come to your senses and try to understand why. It's good if the shock is not very strong, and you are quite hearty, retaining enough reserves for the next attempt. But again—a shock right to the face instead of the promised cheese...

We come to uneasy ground where there are no easy answers—an issue of power. Let's put politics aside for a while and look at what happened with the System that tries to follow some general concept and ignores practical issues in an example of an experiment that I participated in myself.

~ CHAPTER FOUR ~
TWO SIMPLE OPTIONS

In 2017, the "red project," launched exactly 100 years before by the revolution in the Russian empire, came up for discussion. In the 19th century, industrial development finally changed the significance of the means of production. They became large, complex, and too expensive for those who worked them. There appeared on the economic scene the capitalist, who tried to extract from the situation as much as possible at the expense of his employees. For these efforts, ultimately, he was met with a revolution, expropriation, and an attempt to build another System, one without owners, exploitation, and other such unpleasantries.

The basic idea of how to achieve coveted "Liberty, Equality, Fraternity" formed the heart of this new, ideal system as a result of revolution, but this ideal plan had to be fulfilled by far from ideal people. Who could have known they'd screw everything up again? Practical details had to be finalized on the fly, and the result turned out to be far from perfect. It's unlikely to turn out any other way if the correctness of these suppositions is supported by a weighty "That's how it should be" together with a subjugating and punishing state apparatus. The Soviet Union demonstrated impressive military might and progress of government projects without taking into consideration the losses of human lives. For the vast majority that was never a never-ending sacrifice in the name of a better future, which was regularly postponed for the next five years.

So, in the case of the Soviet Union, they took an idea that we liked and decided to prove that they hadn't made a mistake, at any cost. A group of people took up the implementation of it, dictating rules, with which it was better not to argue if you were not interested in a long dispute with KGB officers. Following this concept, they soon began thinking and making decisions for every economic agent. Let's focus on a particular detail: In such a schema, the state acts as a universal seller and a universal buyer. The state decides for everyone what products are useful, how much they should cost, and how much should be produced. In practice, the state becomes a third party to all economic transactions, which have now ceased to be a matter of rational choice for their direct participants.

The state also acts as a common employer in this scenario, deciding how work should be done and how much it is worth. If the work is not completed as it ought to be, the planning and distribution System will not be able to just reject and not pay for it. Dismissing an employee is even more complicated, so the only options left are either punishment for administrative violations or, on occasion, pursuit of a criminal case. The clear, universal rules about which we spoke earlier have, in this schema, become the exclusive domain of state regulation. As a result, the Rubicon—that dividing line behind which things can be managed without the intervention of people with heavy-duty arguments—was wiped away due to uselessness because they expanded their power to all segments of the economy. Now, the state, when writing its rules, has only to check with itself, and everyone else has to accept the result as ordained.

Ordinary people participate in the operation of the System. They have to make a career for themselves and get bonuses, and in order to do this, they must fulfill and surpass the stipulated target. There is one way to make this schema more manageable, and that is to manipulate the requirements for the product itself. The System discovered a new opportunity: It acquired the ability to distort the rules, tweaking them to suit its needs. If the task is too difficult to manage without breaking the rules, then why not just build lies into the rules themselves? There could be nothing simpler—we both write and approve them all on our own.

There is a set of clear requirements that it is difficult to interpret ambiguously. For example, a dairy product everywhere must be made from milk, a meat product from meat. Milk can only be acquired from the mammary glands of mammals and does not occur anywhere else. Meat consists of muscle tissue, not just any type of processed organic matter, whether tinted and stuffed with additives or not. In the case of a state-planned economy, a rigid schema, one that sets for everyone a lower limit regarding what's acceptable, has fallen into the hands of someone who possesses the most heavy-duty arguments, bending to his interests. In place of an accurate and objective statement of the question, produced by specially trained people, we receive from the System ready-made answers that are not always logical, but are suitable for those who currently find themselves on top. They cannot afford to conduct themselves in such a way when it comes to responsible areas; here is where the principle of "at any cost" becomes relevant. It's convenient because "any cost" is divided among everyone in such a centralized System. In other respects, if established requirements interfere with the achievement of planned quotas, the state planner can revise them, at least in those areas where it is not immediately obvious. Everyone else—those who will use or buy the product—for lack of choice, will simply have to adopt it as it is.

The unconditional becomes conditional—sour cream is produced in the amount planned, but, at the same time, it becomes thin and watery, sold in one small glass jar per customer, and it is supposed that this is enough. The permissible number of additives and impurities in products depends on the state of the harvest, the situation with raw materials, and the fulfillment of the plan. Now, finding a flat wall in a panel house is no simple or trivial task because if you take a tape measure, then you realize that a square room is far not so square. But everything that's supposed to be normal by the state is normal.

When the issue is formulated correctly, the value of an industrial product is determined by the utility of its function and the length of its service life, during which useful characteristics are retained in the required amount. There was a specific property of domestic cars and other such complex mechanisms that aroused a particular kind of pride. They were constantly breaking, but rarely completely or for good. Out of two to three half-dead contraptions, it was always possible to assemble one Frankenstein monster capable of lurching forward.

ASKING THE RIGHT QUESTIONS

Back to computers—ours were constantly going out of whack, and we were supposed to be controlling space satellites with these things. A control session might only last all of fifteen minutes, during the course of which at least one of the two contraptions ought not to fail. Our machines behaved like a couple of picky elderly ladies whose whims, especially in the spring, followed along with all the changes in pressure and temperature. Long before the start of the session, we tried to determine which device would be the most capricious that day and to prepare for it. You had to guess what was going wrong by looking at the behavior of the devices and at flashing lights on the console (those machines had no monitors), which displayed binary code - "0" or "1" for each bit of the main processor and controllers.

A solid half of potential malfunctions could be fixed with a light and accurately placed blow to the right spot on a number of printed circuit boards. To levy this blow, we used the shoes that came with the set of uniforms we were provided. Sometimes, just pulling out one component and plugging it back in was enough. Now, imagine rushing from cabinet to cabinet across two auditoriums of 100 square meters each, knocking on racks, pulling and swapping circuit boards, literally using your own two hands to try and force the stalled computing process forward by just a step. Add to this the twenty-four hours on/twenty-four hours off schedule and the threat to get a penalty and lose the one day off per month we were allotted in the event of failure, the polar day and polar night... Well, you can understand now why we needed alcohol so badly.

Somewhere in a parallel dimension, microprocessors already existed. In Hollywood films, people were fighting robots and competing in battles of wits with ruthless machinic minds. On the bright side, nothing like this was threatening us—our "artificial intelligence" was completely helpless without the presence of a shoe in a skillful hand.

In the late 1980s, the correct idea around which the System was built no longer seemed so correct, and the result after seventy years of experimentation named the Soviet Union was unconvincing.

With the fervor of a neophyte, we rushed to the opposite

extreme—to the liberal economy. It seems now the "invisible hand of the market" was at work. The author of this definition, Scottish economist Adam Smith, probably did not see this "hand," because in the 18th century, the logic of rational economic behavior had not been so formalized, and it was believed that everything happened of its own accord. Similarly, the originators of the new liberal experiment in our country didn't see it either, too carried away by unfolding prospects. They spent a great deal of time discussing the idea in general terms, taking delight in the successes of others without paying attention to the mundane details that made this idea work.

It would be naive to expect former citizens of the Soviet Union who tumbled from the distributor to the free market to voluntarily and publicly set the limits of their own responsibility (I'm talking about the rules from the second chapter that set the lower limit beyond which the product cannot be considered valid and therefore cannot be bought or sold). Now the manipulation of the rules is not a move forced by the System in order to fulfill the plan, but a field for profitable compromises available to all.

No one began regulating and limiting themselves, consciously and consistently relying on objective knowledge, even though by doing so there was a good chance to create their own agenda, independent of the state apparatus—practical issues that had to be dealt with on a continuous basis. As a result, all participants began to propose and discuss options that were convenient for themselves while the state retained the final word on matters of regulation. This is how the idea of self-regulation in the economy neutered itself.

Self-regulation, as was understood here, was limited to the revision of one's own old rules or the reproduction of those of others in a way that was seen as convenient. All that emerged from this was an unstable channel for seeking a bureaucratic compromise between the "self-regulating" market agents and the only regulator, the state. The rules that were designed to restrict the flow of anything that shouldn't be on the market (such as fakes and defective merchandise) became an elastic set of conventions that left room open to make a deal. This is how we got a System in which everything is possible, from facile foxiness to shameless lies.

The deformation of the rules does not happen so obviously

and abruptly; a certain inertia is at play, looking back to experience, tradition, and the remnants of common sense. We still have colleagues whose "homework" we can copy. We can look at the social and state structure in different ways, but the natural sciences, mathematics, and physics are right where they've always been, unchanged. Both the support beam and the compressed steam in the boiler are described by the same formulas, regardless of political trends. Accordingly, the rules based on these formulas might change in detail, but their fundamental content will remain the same, independent of the color of the flag and the opinions of ideologues. The standards might look different, but our textbooks are all the same. The logic of description—how does one reproduce a good product?—is not fundamentally different, either.

Under this approach, the contents of technical documents based on objective knowledge cannot in any way differ in meaning or logic from the same standards written by other people in another language as far as we speak about the same practical issue. But in our state apparatus, where you can't swing a dead cat without hitting a lawyer, nobody guessed at this. At first, foreign standards were looked over and were intended to be taken as a model. Then, it was announced that their elephants are quite different from our elephants and that all our ideas about elephants had to undergo a stringent analysis, followed by adaptations and modifications that took into account our particularities, geographical specificities, and cultural heritage.

Later, foreign standards analogs were declared instruments of hostile external interference, hindering the development and implementation of our strategic plans. At least, this is what patriotic manufacturers and the most progressive officials began to say. Now there was nothing to stand in the way of rewriting documents in accordance with the national interest and our unique mentality. A strict and logical schema that will prevent the appearance of "something similar" in lieu of a full-fledged product can be constructed by asking a few well-posed questions. But people who wished to ask those questions could not be found or preferred to keep quiet and not urinate against the wind. That the opportunity for lying is not in the answer, but in the very formulation of the question itself—what will we consider deception?—presents the possibility of remaining half-honest for as long as convenient.

A situation has arisen that can be well explained by the inertia left over from the previous seventy-year experiment. The participants opted for a simple sleight of hand—regulation became a subject of bureaucratic exercises with excessive formalization. It was much easier to pass the paper routine than to solve the technical task itself and explain it to an official. After this, what may be a boring task for a narrow circle of specially trained people who understand the subject has now become a delightful exercise in sophistry. Discussion of the rules has become something of a theological debate, a search for the correct description of something that no one can (or wants to) understand. Because following general patterns described by norms and directives is the easiest way to avoid any responsibility for own decisions.

When in 2014 the Russian state decided to reject all milk from the European Union, it would have been worth remembering that it takes a cow no less than two years to mature, copulate, and finally produce milk. And first, another cow needs to give birth to that one, which doesn't happen right away, either. It is impossible to find quickly thousands of other unemployed cows ready to give the same milk at the same price. But we were promised that this maneuver would be carried out practically free of charge, maintaining prices with the help of prosecutorial, parliamentary, antimonopoly, and supervisory controls. When serious people start to puff out their cheeks and demonstrate confidence, reality sags under pressure. The economics textbook's simple equilibrium of supply and demand is no match for this nonsense!

In a real pinch, instead of a European cow, a Malaysian palm will do. A surefire technology for the replacement of milk with palm oil cannot exist, but there is a solution: With the help of simple sophisms, concepts like "milk" and "dairy product" can be made conditional and flexible.

In April 2016, during a live, nationwide presidential phone-in, farmers complained that their natural milk was being hopelessly outperformed by the industrial production of palm oil surrogates. At a subsequent meeting with government representatives, the question was forwarded to the Minister of Agriculture. From his view, it appeared that the problem was entirely one of correct labeling. To resolve the issue, it was simply necessary to indicate on the packaging the presence of substitutes, which should not, in principle, be included in dairy products. Ultimately, the inscription had to be applied in the correct way, coordinating the font and size with other EurAsEC partners. The Deputy Prime Minister then chimed in with his expert opinion, stating that sometimes substitutes can even be good for children. The speakers described their sophisticated view of a simple issue with the characteristic expression of a person who doesn't believe very strongly in what they are saying. Like a D student at the blackboard, they mumbled some words that were appropriate in meaning and waited tensely, hoping the teacher wouldn't rephrase the question in such a way that they would be forced to answer it clearly and directly.

It remains a mystery how, in the years following the imposition of the embargo, the production of dairy products could grow at such a shocking pace even though the total number of livestock did not increase. It also took many years to agree on the size and font of the inscription that would indicate how much milk could be milked from one palm tree.

All these rules, standards, and descriptions of processes and products are necessary for organizing interaction and producing results with the System. The economy is arranged such that someone will always end up paying for error or deceit. When we turn to substitution in the writing of these management tools, losses are inevitable. Then the System no longer determines the source of the problem, it simply divides the costs among everyone or shifts them to those less fortunate than others.

~ CHAPTER FIVE ~
THE PRICE OF COMPROMISE

In economic planning, there is the concept of net present value (NPV). We build a sequence of events, evaluate the effects of each in terms of money, and multiply this amount by the probability that the event will occur. All in all, we get a series that predicts our final result. Everything is more or less clear when it comes to money, but probability assessments are typically more complicated. Part of the risk is related to the fact that any operation involves "subjects with limited rationality," that is, ordinary people who might make mistakes or cheat.

In the second chapter, we talked about the tools that make it possible to manage these risks, helping to bring the buyer's expectations and the seller's capabilities into closer alignment. In the course of an experiment on the implementation of an exciting idea—a planned distribution economy—the state decided for both participants in the transaction. In Russia, we built the next experiment around the concept of the "free market," copying it in its broadest strokes. The risk management tools, which were also slapped together without much attention to detail, left enough loopholes for participants' "limited rationality" to manifest.

We deform the rules that are used to organize our economic interactions: Where they might be rigid and clear, we replace them with conventionality dependent on the position of certain people and inevitable compromises. The schema on which the engagement of participants is built is slowly beginning to unravel. The cut-off line—that "rock bottom" that ensures that everything the rules define as an unsuitable product remains behind it—"floats" somewhere in the middle. The lack of a tool capable of clearly recognizing error or fraud negates all the advantages that come from specialization and division of labor. So, bit by bit, we lose the opportunity to plan our tomorrow.

One need only allow a small substitution in the writing or "adaptation" of the standards and rules, replacing direct and comprehensible formulations with something more convenient for the more foolhardy subjects with limited rationality to rush in and fill this tiny gap. They'll force their way through the boundaries of the permissible until these boundaries are completely abolished. Those who went in for a "little gimmick" with actual quality in the very beginning, now establish associations of the "almost honest," and "more or less honest," explaining how their products are better without admitting where they themselves lied. They all move away from straightforward formulations of the question, wriggling their way out of providing transparent answers, dwelling instead in the relative categories of "better" or "worse." It no longer bothers anyone when in contracts or public offers something like "...products must conform to all the highest standards of quality..." becomes a habitual refrain. More often than not, this means products need not conform to anything.

In matters of quality, there are no longer trustworthy arbitrators capable of providing clear and direct answers and removing everything from the market that shouldn't be there. Instead, each of us needs to acquire our own home chemical laboratory along with the knowledge and skills of all these "specially trained people." As far as most statements and labels about quality became just declarations without any actual background, we must do a deep dive into all the intricacies of food production, things, repairs, and even medicine with the assistance of acquaintances, the Internet, and television programs and look for a solution ourselves.

Nevertheless, the Russian state remains the final authority in matters of quality. In the chapter about "clear rules," we spoke about the professional formulation of the question, when "quality" isn't an excuse to talk but a defined set of measurement indicators. We've replaced these indicators, which can be measured, calculated, and proved with convention, the subject of compromise with those who decide "how it should be." State regulators, on the one hand, periodically select the "highest quality" from an array of the "not so high quality" and just create fuss and additional expenditures without actually solving any problems.

If we aren't talking about an individual deal, but trying to organize a complex process, realized by a group of people who intend to do something together, yet at the same time each will decide on their own what they can't do so that the common plan doesn't fall apart. Everyone will act as their own life experience, opinion, and assessment of the situation prompts them to, cutting corners on the details they consider insignificant. To start: On planning and design. Then: On the choice of components or materials, on everything not immediately visible to the eye. Some might forget about allowance or processing accuracy, others about additives or what kind of solder must be used in a rocket engine... I've witnessed many times how projects worth millions of dollars become risky ventures simply because someone decided to try to "save" a few thousand.

All that remains to be done is to rely on objectivity, common decency, goodwill, and other such nebulous concepts. One person does their job, then another one comes along to mess everything up just following his own interest in certain steps of a common project. Nobody actively objects; at the next stage, they hope to turn the tables so that everyone gets the chance to put things back the way they prefer. Management is structured in such a way that everyone has the opportunity to explain that they did everything "as stipulated," which they'll confirm by manipulating the numerous corresponding documents.

As we approach the finale of the whole project, we can say with certainty that the result will be far from expected. The cautious parties pull back, trying to keep what they've already gained. The question is how miserable the outcome will turn out to be, and whether the participants will be able to find a way out of the sticky position into which they've placed themselves. They'll walk a balance beam between the hope of making it to the end and the need to flee, hauling off as much as they can, until their secrets, both big and small, come to light. For those who remain, work meetings come to seem like a game of poker or the final showdown from a Tarantino film. Everyone's acting buddy-

buddy, but, at the same time, being paranoid and villainous. Under the table, everyone's holding each other at gunpoint or trying to poke at each other's weak spots.

Words, whether spoken or written on paper lying in plain sight, mean little. Participants would rather try to scare each other with the importance and complexity of the task than try to understand and think through it together. The main question is never spoken aloud: Who will remain at the table for the next round and who will get what? Who will get the money, and who will receive the payback for their own mistakes and those of others? The first candidate for "departure" is the "overachiever" – usually the most ambitious or less experienced player. He'll rush forward and take upon himself all the blunders, pay for all the assumptions and ambiguous interpretations. If he's lucky enough and strong enough, he'll make it to the end. But more likely, his corpse and interim results will become fodder for savvier finalists.

Following the general "market idea," we copy the "market" optimization tools like auctions and tendering, which were not used in a planned economy. But tools are only useful if they're applied correctly. These procedures are effective so long as they are based on a strict schema that decisively blocks entry to "extra" participants and only allows full-fledged proposals to compete. We let pass all "suitable" comers, guided by a set of formal features and simultaneously complicating this set and all procedures to a level of complete meaninglessness. As a result, our market optimization tools become useless, and more often they work according to a logic of negative or worsening selection. We don't choose the cheapest of the available full-fledged options but rifle through everything, down to proposals that, in an objective analysis, belong in the trash. Then we happily report on the successes we've achieved in imaginary optimization and cost savings.

When we establish such tender procedures, we are seeking the cheapest solution the certain practical tasks and have to come up with informal, real requirements for bidding participants. It's only possible if we understand the subject of the procedure itself. It's necessary to adhere to the algorithm for solving this problem rather than a formal procedure, such that later it will be possible to assemble all of the parts into a unified whole. Then you won't have to rely on the "Blonde Principle," which can let you down and turn the participants into asses.

A colleague of mine supplied his products to the construction site of a large pharmaceutical concern in Altai in southern Siberia. The tender procedures to select contractors went flawlessly, but the result turned out completely predictably—everything broke down during the course of installation. None of the participants had paid attention to the lack of calculations in the project that might have suggested what the breaking strength of the purchased structures needed to be. The client had a decent bunch of lawyers who quickly chose my friend to be the one to blame for everything. A competition began in the production of meaningless tests, written volumes filled with tables and color illustrations, excerpts from Wikipedia, and sentences that had no meaning in terms of technology and common sense. Most striking was the conclusion, made by an expert with an impressive set of diplomas and certificates. He authoritatively stated that relying on the strength of materials theory in solving this problem was as good as relying on Hammurabi's Code. It was impressive that the expert knew the name of the King of Babylon, which left written laws thirty-seven centuries ago, but a dozen people with diplomas lacked precisely an understanding of the task at the level of a school physics course and that was the actual reason for the overall failure of the project. Having lost three years and a lot of money writing useless papers, all that remained was to come to an agreement and close the case with a payment of one single ruble.

If we get to the point of litigation, then it becomes a retrospective attempt to sort out issues that had been ignored unanimously by everyone from the very start. The weightiest arguments are deployed, and the question is resolved "by the code": He who is right is right. Having warped our rules with compromises, we have ourselves made certain there's nothing on which to base counterarguments. A person from the state organs is out of the running here—they can't be wrong. They're endowed with the gift of representing the interests of all their fellow citizens, including orphans and the disabled. Full of responsibility, they can work up a storm in any courtroom, all while maintaining the necessary intonations. The opponent, defending their own personal interest and a party on a smaller scale, is left to make one final mistake. Instead of adhering to a logical and consistent argument where possible, they try to bargain and reach a compromise.

Something of this sort happened in an arbitration proceeding in St. Petersburg. At every attempt to find meaning and logic in the reasoning and arguments of the plaintiff, a state monopolist, the judge let out a loud screech, pounded on the table, and threatened to summon the bailiffs, impose a fine for disrespect, conclude the proceedings, remove the current speaker, reflect this in the protocols, cut off their head... It was quite similar to the trial of the Knave of Hearts who stole those tarts. I participated as an expert on behalf of the defendant and tried to insist on applying a technical solution to what was a technical problem, without resorting to dramatics or sophistry. I tried to explain the issue in terms of the school's physical textbook and as a result, I was evicted from the room under threat of a fine for disrespecting the high court. All I managed to finally say to the judge after another round of rebukes, threats, and explications, was, "Take care."

That's how we built a market where there are neither rules nor obligations that must be carried out to the end, although there are lots of opportunities to sort things out "by the code." It's a market where the state regulator can again participate in practically every transaction, either vertically or horizontally, just like in the planned economy. At the same time, their participation doesn't contribute towards the solution of the main issue: ensuring operations safety and increasing the chances of producing the desired outcome. We still have to work "by feeling": Correct and rational decisions are usually achieved by trial and error, without recourse to the actions of the useless regulator.

The realization of any project becomes complicated. Participants must initially deal with constant problems related to the supply of raw materials and components, or else start acting like everyone else and switch to "something similar."

When there is no System capable of reliably identifying surrogates, then real products either abandon such a market or never enter it in the first place. Suppliers of real products are forced to compete not with peers but with everyone offering "something almost exactly the same, but a little cheaper." The task of those entering such a market with a fully realized product is many times more difficult than that of less principled players.

This, however, is not the biggest problem. These days, if necessary, you can quickly compensate for the lack of any material resources. There remains what is the most important and most sensitive issue that cannot be speedily rectified with the help of simple manipulations.

Do you recall the question "What do they need from me?" that we each ask the System and ourselves in the first place? At least seven hours a day, approximately two hundred to two hundred forty days—in total, one and a half thousand hours of our lives per year—we exchange for money. How much is this hour worth and how many hours can we sell? What do we need to know and be able to do, and how much additional effort will be required to sell this product at a higher rate? Can this product be protected from counterfeiting? What happens when people are missing support or adequate feedback from the System?

As a next logical step System does not recognize a specialist who has the necessary knowledge and practical skills and does not protect them from other applicants who have offered a lower price but are only able to offer "something similar" instead of real labor.

Sometimes many of them get lost.

~ CHAPTER SIX ~
"LOST BOYS"

There's one worthwhile thought in that fairytale about angry Atlanteans by Ayn Rand. There is no lousy work; lousy work is done by lousy people. But how can you tell good work from bad if nobody is willing or able to accept any responsibility? The desire to simplify your life is completely natural. Those same mechanisms that make it possible to replace a product with a surrogate also make it possible to replace a person who knows how to do something with others who agree to try their hand at it and will do it cheaper.

When the schema for evaluating results—finished products—began to warp, the logic for evaluating the qualifications of those creating products also began to "drift." Just as we've found a way to eliminate operations necessary for the manufacture of a full-fledged product or to replace them with meaningless pieces of paper, we've also made the education, skills, and experience of those performing these operations "superfluous."

In 2016, I asked a taxi driver from Chita, a city in Eastern Siberia, about the Chinese economic presence there, as the border is very close.

"There were lots of Chinese folks, but now almost all of them have left."

"What were they doing here?"

"Building housing."

"For themselves?"

"No, for us, of course. For them, there was only half-brick temporary barracks..."

"And what were you up to at that time?"
"We did business."
"What kind?"
"You know what kind. The women were selling junk, and the men guarded the women..."

Four years later, I was watching a TV news report about how a spring hurricane in that very same Chita had blown the roofs off houses there and how by October they still had not been repaired. Rain flowed freely across the upper floors. I had not thought to ask the taxi driver if, with the departure of the Chinese, the community had lost anything else of value. Had they also taken away the locals' desire and ability to build and repair their own houses?

At a conference, a representative of the Ministry of Labor spoke at length and in great detail about how the writing and approval of detailed instructions led to a reduction in injuries at construction sites. In passing, there was some mention of data from a study that had been conducted: At the time of the survey, 30 percent of workers coming to the construction site had documents confirming they had the necessary qualifications, while another 40 percent stated they were learning "on the job." The final 30 percent had gotten lost somewhere in the report. And although the presenter had already moved on to conclusions and prospects, he admitted, after a follow-up question, that in a number of cases the respondents had dispersed too quickly to apprehend like cockroaches in a kitchen when a light switched on when inspectors arrived on the construction site. In the instances when it had been possible to find or catch them, it had been too difficult to capture accurate data due to translation difficulties. Questions remain: How do these 30 percent read and understand these rules and how is the technical task explained to them? What is the final result of such construction work?

Complex issues are formed from simple ones. For example, a secondary technical education for builders implies the ability to read blueprints and understand what not to do, even if the boss is not breathing down the employee's neck right at that moment. What metamorphosis relegated this skill to the category of the worthless, dismissed even literacy as unnecessary, and made it possible to replace technical competence with a small bunch of primitive management tools—a capacious set of obscene words, universal interjections, and gestures?

Although it's worth crossing the border and verifying that in countries with a much higher GDP per person, citizens there don't disdain this kind of work at all. But okay. Let's suggest for a moment that the work we've just discussed is simple and "dirty," perfectly fine to leave to guest laborers. Let's go up a level and see what's happening in places where people with higher technical education typically work.

Consider earthquakes and construction in quake zones.

For the layman, an earthquake is a catastrophe, a disaster: People run screaming, and everything in the area collapses and is destroyed. For the specialist, these are loads, stresses, and strains expressed in kilograms and meters, or pounds and inches. In the first instance, this is a good reason to be scared and to scare others. In the second, it's a comprehensible task for which a solution can be found by evaluating the seismic activity and accounting for it in calculations.

If the engineer solves the problem correctly, then within a given probability the first instance will be prevented entirely.

In our instance, it's easier to use traditional solutions, approved at the time of the Soviet Union. We can pull something appropriate and similar from the ranks of the "tried and true," and pass through clearances and approvals. But what if you've got something new to offer and you want to break the mold? As an example, I tried to apply new solutions for construction on mountain slopes in preparation for the Sochi 2014 Winter Olympic Games. The first thing authorities demanded from me to approve my offers was a certificate stating that my product met all the requirements stipulated in regulations having to do with earthquakes, and they even showed me a few examples "in confidence." It turns out that this constitutes sufficient proof, and no calculations are necessary. By contrast, when I showed up with calculations and proposed that they be verified, I ended up creating a ton of problems for everyone—myself most of all. The calculations were set aside, and I was asked for "real proof," which is to say, something impressive, on a form with some seals, which can then be placed into a file of documents to reestablish certitude and equilibrium. Furthermore, this kind of "indulgence" won't run me more than twenty thousand rubles or four hundred US dollars. Loads need not be determined—they'll be supported (or born) by a numbered form on a wonderful piece of paper. But, in reality, all it verifies and confirms is that the people who filled out and approved this certificate are not doing their jobs, just because they do not understand —what are they doing at all?

It's a simple trick you're encouraged to pull, with the substitution of a technical task with a meaningless document masquerading as the solution. So, you take as co-authors the entire System and the writers of its approved templates at once, while you'll be responsible for your own thought-out and calculated version yourself. If you try very hard, you might still be able to find a specialist capable of building a calculation model. But finding them will be about as easy as finding a unicorn in the town park.

The participation of a professional is economically justified when they can find the best option to be implemented in the resolution of a concrete task. But if no one presents the task in this manner? No, they just constantly natter on about cost optimization, preferring to keep quiet about how the project can be completed after budget cuts and altering plans to fit with more familiar forms. Testing centers, stands where calculations are verified and proof is found, are falling into disrepair. They're being replaced by a printer spitting out empty but "correct" papers. What's demanded is not a solution, but documentation that will satisfy inspectors. It'll also contain the best excuse for any occasion: "We did everything in accordance with standards and legislation...!"

We got used to relying on software products to resolve engineering questions quite quickly, almost forgetting that they're just tools. They'll only provide the correct result if they're being used by an engineer who knows what they're doing. In that case, the tools will help the engineer, but in no way will they replace said engineer.

At the very beginning of our project, I encountered another "specific" local problem. Designers were trained on a basis inherited from the planned economy when they usually made a choice between several permitted options without any attempt to optimize a project and preferred only options with all the collected approvals. In practice, the issue of structural reliability became a rather formal part of design. Such calculations were actually left to sellers to resolve as part of the product's promotion. Salesmen tried to slip their own materials into the project and presented options for the use of their products in ways that were most beneficial to themselves. In their own "fast and loose" interpretation, suppliers are not at all restricted in anything; the main thing is that the bottom line shows a positive result. That's enough to procure an approval, and nobody will check how realistic the projections are. Such solutions turn out to be extremely optimistic, primarily due to the neglect of important details that shouldn't be overlooked when modeling an actual project. So, I tried to perform the role of such a seller, but I quickly realized that I wasn't going to be able to outwit my competitors. I lacked acting skills.

My supervisor explained that throughout the world, three known and popular methods of static calculation were used like this: American, German, and French. All three options were based on the same logic, but I was not able to read the French one. My colleague proposed to use the German method, which he knew best. It furthermore took into account important details that resulted in a more exact calculation model than the American approach.

I took up the translation. A couple years later, a Russian version of the methodology and a program based on it were published. I hoped that these tools would help establish full-fledged calculations instead of the wiles of advertising as the basis for design decisions. That hope was in vain. Quickly, I saw that only a few experts and designers demonstrated any interest, and salesmen of construction products continued doing calculations as before, just using my program like a new toy. They entered data that exceeded the boundaries of common sense and overestimated indicators by dozens or even hundreds of times, none of which was picked up by the software. On the other hand, no tragedy happened. Calculations remained a formality that few people paid any attention to, just another stack of paper covered in scribbles.

A simple algorithm able to recognize and evaluate a specific product—a qualification or a quality human resource—cannot be founded solely on the creation of laws and standards or on an increase in the army of inspectors and "inspectors of inspectors." No program, certificate, or attestation can be substituted for the ability of a person to understand what they're doing. Otherwise, one must either assign additional inspectors or coordinators or else wait and see where this substitution process leads. More than once, I've seen how these inspectors, at the sight of a foolish error, simply blink and demand that a paper be brought, or at least composed, on which it states clearly that said error is, in fact, an error.

You can launch an endless number of showcases with competitions and awards, and bureaucratic exercises with certification processes, but the results will be zilch—the logic giving meaning to the whole performance is nowhere to be found.

As a result, the requirements for determining a specialist's qualifications are constructed according to one of two methods:

- I have the necessary piece of paper and can find or guess the correct document that contains the correct word, line, column—everything that might pass as an answer. This is despite the fact that I can't even formulate the question to which I'm providing the answer. I can do something similar in any situation and can try to convince everyone that this is how it should be. And, generally speaking, I don't ask for much.

Or:

- I'm ready to describe the main requirements of my work and to prove to any of those "in the know" that trying to evade these requirements just means they're deceiving themselves. I'm ready to go to bat for and to discuss the fairness of my requests, but only with those who understand the stakes of the issues. Finally, I know how to do this job, having fulfilled all requirements to the end, I can do it, and if it turns out I've lied, then you can withhold payment.

The second option should be the norm. Most often, however, on unveiling the results of the work and removing all its "wrapping," we'll find the first. What should be the norm becomes the exception. The trained person who is worth asking for a solution and paying money for this service loses their place. They are replaced with an imitator or a simpler, inexpensive formal procedure.

It's easiest to attribute the problem to the abandonment of the "correct" planned system and careless "liberalization." But liberalization has precisely nothing to do with it. In a planned economy, conditions were set by the System in a direct, non-alternative manner. Barring realignment and simplification, it couldn't do things differently by force of objective reasons. Liberalization didn't mean a total lack of regulation, but rather that the participants themselves had to solve these issues to the best of their abilities and professionalism.

It didn't work out that way.

Yes, now the hours of our lives are a commodity. Maybe that sounds provocative, but the economy doesn't know any other form of relationship. If we accept this arrangement as necessary, then it becomes important for each of us to know and understand its conditions: How we ought to fill this hour, where and how to sell it for the highest price.

Dear professionals: If you have tried so consistently to reduce the complexity of your labor to the simple reflex of signing and sealing, to the level of a trained monkey, then why are you so surprised when the proffered pay for this work is a banana? What do you know and what can you do to make your labor worth more?

If the trick of substituting rules provides freedom from inconvenient limitations, then there is no need for an employee who knows, understands, and is capable of fulfilling these requirements. Real technologists, welders, designers, and so on are unnecessary. Anyone with an understanding of what must be done only complicates the process of trading in promises on which, in the final tally, no one will fully deliver. Knowledge and experience become redundant, unnecessary baggage. Specialists are gradually disappearing due to a lack of demand.

Instead of mourning lost and departed geniuses, we might think about an equally valuable unit that as of now is worth almost nothing. This unit is the person who has performed a certain job for three to five years and has done it acceptably (not least because it paid well). These types are now an endangered species about whom we must worry at least as much as we do about the emigration of our most intelligent and talented workers. To prevent the continued erosion of this resource, the System must learn to recognize and differentiate it from counterfeits, just like with any other product. Otherwise, it'll be replaced by a different one: "Lost" people who have learned a little something and worked a little while under somebody.

The worth of the slice of our life that we must sell now depends more on the situation, our acquaintances, connections, and many other conditions that do not have objective value rather than on what we really know and can do. In a circle of close liaisons, anyone could be considered a specialist. Drive 50, 100, 200 kilometers away, and without proximity ties, you're no longer a specialist but just another person with what might as well be a fake ID (certificate, credential). Until you prove otherwise, your price is about half of what might be considered fair. So, in this manner we limit mobility and even further reduce the chances of survival for professionals.

Negative selection operates on the same logic at the level of organizations. It's unsurprising that, as a result, the winning hand lies not with those who produce the outcome, but with those who know how to divvy it up. The closer to the cash register, the fewer complicated rules—just arithmetic and the ability to be in the right place at the right time. Companies "burdened" with too detailed an understanding of their obligations are the first to sink. These are quickly replaced by empty shells created for a certain budget expenditure. It isn't necessary to retain specialists and form well-functioning teams for this purpose.

If there are no functional safeguards able to detect imposters and protect real professionals at all levels of complexity, Atlanteans, and geniuses, with their strategic plans, can hide out in their forbidden valley, covering themselves with a cunning, protective umbrella as suggested by Ayn Rand in the novel mentioned above. There will be no one around to bring their great plans to fruition and, most importantly, no one to whom they might sell these fruits.

Champions will always be unique; that's why they're champions. The difference between the "chosen one" and those who would take their place is, almost always, a fraction of a percent. A leader's position is pointless if there isn't anyone breathing down their neck. The foundation consists of the majority—people who work, at minimum, at the average anticipated level, trying to rise a little higher. If it doesn't work out, then either they've got to change jobs or reevaluate their self-image. Without this kind of scaffolding, we sink into a swamp filled with warm and convenient compromises. These compromises destroy that part of the System that creates the working conditions for the majority of professionals—the part that can be built by following clear, universal rules.

Now, let's move a step higher, from special tasks to management proper. To those people who do not take anything heavy into their own hands, because their job is to lead others. Here, substitutions and loss of the actual subject of the job can go even further, and it is even more difficult to recognize the actions of the people who usually represent the System itself.

~ CHAPTER SEVEN ~
MIMICS

In the late '60s, a puppet cartoon called *The Little Goat Who Counted to Ten* premiered in the Soviet Union. The protagonist loudly called out to those around him and assigned everyone a number. He did it without permission and no one appreciated the goat's initiative. At a critical moment, when the boat on which the little goat and his antagonists found themselves began to sink, the goat was permitted to name and number everyone on board. What followed was a miraculous rescue, catharsis, and a general recognition of the protagonist's outstanding talents. From that moment on, the goat began to assign everyone a name and number, and they began to respect and obey him for this.

This story inspired vague doubts in me even before I began school and encountered Archimedes' principle of buoyant force. The little goat just shouted out names and numbers—and lo, order was established, and the problem was solved. None of the passengers were thrown overboard and none of them even moved to another locale, but, for some reason, the boat stopped sinking (obviously, the screenwriter was Team Goat). It seems that some people imagine the majority of managerial problems can be solved by simply finding the right combination of names and numbers and presenting that in a convincing manner.

Let's call them Mimics.

The poorer a System is organized, the sooner it forgets what it was organized for in the first place. Everyone is so busy searching for a way to hold on to their positions or to snag higher ones that their connection to the general task becomes blurred—that same task that ought to justify the existence of the System. How your efforts look from above becomes more important than the end result, and there are more and more chances that the System will begin to work for itself.

Mimics receive exceptional advantages in such a System. When a specialist writes the rules, they are bound by the parameters of their own competence. They'll reach a particular limit and recognize that the assumptions and qualifications that have been undertaken might now become a source of new problems and the tools at their disposal are not adequate to the task of solving the problem with the necessary accuracy. And at this point, the specialist will lose to the person who simply knows how to make a better impression.

The "goat scholar" successfully combines images, calls them by the right smart words, and thereby lends them the appearance of a meaningful solution or plan. They're not constrained by the need to construct complete chains of logic and to find supporting evidence. After all, they aren't looking for an actual result but for approval from their superiors. And if the boss sees a reflection of their own brilliant idea in the proposed imitation, then that's a real success.

Where a specialist will limit themselves to one, or a maximum of five, requirements that will be strung together by logic, necessary, and sufficient, the goat scholar will come up with ten and keep going. This special gibberish of rounded and often illogical formulations furnishes our scholar with endless possibilities. Confidence in the magical power of the correct, properly ordered words propels them forward. A convincing presentation and design become much more important than logic and content, and, where a specialist must solve a problem, the Mimic proposes their own version to shore it up with the necessary "That's how it should be." Properly filled-out documents, over which the Mimic can carry out the rituals of clearance and approval, are suitable for this purpose. After these ceremonies, the System confers upon the texts an almost sacred meaning and designates them the source of all correct answers. It's just that genuine solutions for actual problems can rarely ever be found there.

In a neighboring department or ministry, fellow Mimics will

also try to cook something up on the same topic. One will be incompatible with the other, but this won't be confusing for anyone besides those unlucky losers who will have to follow these rules. Blueprints will be functionally useless, but not to worry—those same boring specialists will be the ones to answer for any failure. Breaking the rules becomes a natural consequence stemming from the fact that they're written by people who don't need to understand what's at stake. Once laid down, approved, and signed, the rules don't really work but create a virtual reality where everything goes according to the established order, goals are achieved, and everything remains under control. We find out what is happening in this parallel universe through large, representative meetings—plenums and forums—and hear from the media. How things are going in the real world, we see from the contents of our wallets.

In the 19th century, two great Germans, Karl Marx and Max Weber, had a discussion about the figure of the bureaucrat. Karl Marx saw this inhabitant of a large and complex control System as the source of evil; Max Weber saw a useful, functional unit. The bureaucrat makes sure that everything remains "within parameters," remaining useful and inoffensive, so long as these "parameters" are established by those who understand the meaning of what's going on around them and can subordinate bureaucratic procedure to the aims of solving a common problem. Disaster occurs when the bureaucrat has the opportunity to be creative in their work. When the Mimic undertakes to write the rules, he creates such opportunities one after the other. Now the executable algorithm is transformed into an inexhaustible source of contradictions that can be understood and interpreted by a whim. When bureaucrats begin to do this, or, even better, when they begin to create rules for themselves, then an ideal breeding ground for raising the bureaucrat's population is established.

Many times, while working, I have been obliged to get approval for new technical solutions from the Russian authorities. The System's initial answer is almost always negative—the solution doesn't conform to the requirements of one or another regulation. I had been prepared to believe this until I decided to delve into the contents of these documents myself. It became clear that my opponents didn't read them and didn't care to understand them. Instead, they rifled through them in search of phrases that can be used as direct instructions or, at least, hints about what can and cannot be done. A negative answer almost always means that they've been unable to find the right phrases and they have, as is their habit, decided to take up a safe, defensive stance.

In any hierarchical structure in which the imperative "That's how it should be" outweighs common sense, this process will begin with equal success. This will provoke attempts to circumvent or cheat the fundamental laws of economics or the natural sciences—everything that's useless to try to deceive. For market players, the need to pay for such a trick appears quickly—they run out of money and opportunities. With the state, the biggest and most powerful hierarchy, created to solve large-scale, complex problems of a higher order, it's more difficult. The management pyramid grinds away at them so long as it has the required resources.

At the end of 2016, after an analysis of recent troubles, the System received a directive from the very top of the Russian government ordering it to finalize the Technical Regulation on the Safety of Buildings and Structures, to bring it in line with current projects, and to report back in February of next year.

The relevant ministry issued seventeen pages of amendments and three pages of clarifications for said amendments to the law, which itself already spanned thirty-three pages. In the ministry's opinion, in order to comply with the law and restore order, it would be mandatory to comply with the documents they call building codes and comply with all additional building norms and standards being voluntary.

All the institutions, ministries, and departments participating in this discussion issued, in response, another eleven conclusions stating that the Ministry of Construction's amendments could not be ratified because they are contradictory and incorrect. The main problem was that Russia joined the Customs Union and the Union's regulations, which already dealt with this topic using different words that didn't fall into line with the vocabulary of the Ministry of Construction. The glossary is generally a stumbling block occupying a good third of the total number of smart words in these conclusions. The Ministry of Industry and

Trade gave an original performance, assembling a commission of thirty-three experts who didn't waste words and simply majority voted that the bill does not serve the interests of the national economy, its stage of development, generally recognized international standards, and "everything else."

    This resembles an effort to resolve a technical issue in the same manner that was used hundreds, even thousands, of years ago, as if there does not exist any knowledge giving us a full understanding of the questions or any of the tools accumulated by humankind to solve them. We must find or write a text that we can take to be canonical (sacred). Then, we have to turn to it for the answer to every question and argue endlessly, without any practical meaning, about the correct interpretation.

    About a hundred years ago, humanity began proving the reliability of structures via calculation. Everyone who understands the big picture will solve the problem in the same way—in the Russian Federation, in the Customs Union, and beyond. This requires specialists who understand how to formulate the conditions of a task and how to then solve it; that is, to confirm that the load-bearing beam will not collapse before the estimated fifty years with a probability and margin of safety no less than what was specified. Another specialist is required to check the first and to evaluate their work. It doesn't particularly matter whether it's done on a mandatory basis per the boss's order, under threat of punishment, or voluntarily. The primary thing is that the specialists resolve the technical issue without substituting any of the necessary actions with links from one document to another or with the signatures of important and authoritative figures. It's pretty simple, but then 80 percent of all discussions, rituals, and canonical texts would lose all meaning!

    Most representatives don't understand what's at stake and don't want to admit it. They look for ways to solve problems immediately for the country at large by writing laws and issuing orders, relying on the experiences and abstract judgments of respectable people, as they did centuries ago. Voting is an essential part of the process, where the position of directly involved players is taken as the basis, adding to this those who genuinely agree or those expecting to get their palm greased in return. Authorities in science can be invited to add an air of gravitas; they'll say everything that their encyclopedic erudition will permit them, avoiding uncomfortable but correctly posed questions. If they allow such stupidity and start asking such questions, then they simply won't be asked to attend the next Council of the Wise.

You can even appeal to common sense, a school physics textbook. That you will find yourself in the same company as Robert Hooke, Isaac Newton, and others mentioned in physics textbooks might give you some solace, but... you're in the minority. The Council of the Wise nonetheless issues another canon, which, after the ritual of affirmation, can be cited and put forth as hard evidence. It's weighty in the literal sense: Nothing boosts confidence and alleviates worry like an impressive stack of scribbled-on paper with seals and signatures on every sheet.

When the formulation is really bad, there's another option. Just make a list or an omnibus of what ought to be considered correct. The logic and principles of formation will be extremely vague and inherited rather from the planned economy. The list will include terminology and nomenclature, but it will forget to specify the technical conditions under which products were made, or else it will indicate product "adaptations" or "placeholder" standards. Remember how reliability doesn't matter at all? That is to say, you can write any combination of numbers and letters on the label, like on a wooden fence, and nobody will require proof; they'll just choose what's cheapest and wait and see what happens, confident that everything's been done "how it should be." After all, that's what it says on paper!

The art of choosing the right words results in unlimited possibilities. It won't be difficult to obtain an analog to any product; we'll apply the term "analog" to whatever we deem necessary. Everything is determined by the Stanislavsky system. An error is when the regulator says, "I don't believe you." In order for them to believe, we have to find citations and excerpts from documents with the required familiar phrases, paste and affix them with links and protocols, and then try to drag the resultant verbal compilation onto a real task, like forcing a square peg into a round hole, pretending that this is how it should be.

All kinds of fashionable methods can be applied to improve and enhance all that we're hardly able to manage. The Mimic, with the right set of words, will be unrivaled in their ability to pass for a technocrat. The icing on the cake is digital modeling or Kaizen, KPI, PSI, and hundreds of other ways to produce a graph in a colorful, motivational presentation, showing growth in the direction of something. Trainers on the implementation of yet another ingenious technique will also be correct in their own way. All of these efforts may, in fact, bring about some effect, but by the same token, we're simply looking for ways to carry water in leaky buckets. We try running faster or grabbing more, but there's no discussion of plugging the holes that we made by numerous compromises with common sense.

These are good tools that serve to increase the efficiency of the basic schema in which everyone understands what needs to be done. Without this basis, the tools become useless and even dangerous. After all, they can't think for people and can't correct an error within the very formulation of the task—what actually has to be done by the humans who use these templates. Blind faith in the undoubted advantages and benefits of using such standard and popular management solutions will just lead us to do new and different stupid things.

A thousand clever words will be spoken instead of looking for an actual solution. There's no time for trifles—the conversation is about state interests, innovations, and development strategies. The biggest fear of speakers is not a practical mistake; it is a threat of losing the most important thing: a place in the hierarchy. One's current place must rather be preserved and parleyed into a better position, closer to the person who sits at the head. All that's needed for this is to generate an unceasing stream of buzzwords, tracking from the corner of your eye the reaction of the primary spectator (provided they are present). This person with authority will decide what is correct and what is wrong. Here, the laws of physics, mathematics, and economics no longer play any role.

It's of utmost importance not to miss a nod or a raised eyebrow, the slightest grimace that turns projects upside down and ends careers. This detail is enough to nullify all preceding calculations and supporting data, shifting everything from the equilibrium of supply and demand to the center of a gravitational pull.

Yes, it's hardly the 21st century—it's the late Middle Ages. We've gone back four hundred years, to the time before Johann

Kepler and Sir Anthony Dean, when we still couldn't understand and didn't even try to use measurements and calculations. Then any issue could be resolved by saying "That's how it should be" and stamping your foot, and when the most complex problems of all were best sorted out by the Pope in Rome.

We've now made it to those directly involved in setting the rules determining "how it should be." We've created the ideal environment for the half-honest players. There's just one step left before the System can also make them half-guilty and how it happens is a subject of the next chapter.

~ CHAPTER EIGHT ~
A TASTE FOR BLOOD

Sans practice, my facility with German quickly dropped to the level of "dictionary-assisted," and the first time I heard the idiom "*hat Blutgeleckt*" it hurt my ears. Especially as it was used in conversation by a woman in every respect the head of an international holding with which I was desperately trying to get a job. Taken literally, it sounds like "licked the blood," although in reality it just means to take a lively interest in something.

Now is a perfect moment to remember that we're talking about algorithms for managing economic processes, and everything costs money here. Rules limit the ability of the human individual to behave as their own physiology directs them. We'll take not just one such individual, but the state itself as a separate group with its own internal hierarchy and disciplines, and we'll endow this group with exclusive powers to establish order. If the nature of this order is known only in its most general outline, then the group members establishing it have room to improvise and, where possible, to size up any outsider from the point of view of that same physiology. What will happen to the medium of power, the wielder of the weightiest arguments, when they come to understand their possibilities in terms of creating rules and restrictions, when they evaluate the number of potential violators and get a... "taste for blood"?

We discussed how rules that had to be rigid and clear became elastic and controversial. The state settled itself in this "twilight zone" in the manner that was most convenient for it. State representatives now became the exclusive bearers of order, the System itself, the only ruler among the ruled. Gradually, the state began to recuperate those regulatory and managerial powers that might prove of great interest to its representatives. Objections and even protests would do nothing to fundamentally alter this situation. Ruled economic subjects could only accept a ready-made version of an order from the state because they didn't want to work on one of their own.

In such a situation, state representatives can alter the rules as they like. But even if the rules themselves don't change, they can interpret them in any number of ways, since there are so many, and they're written in such a vague way as to encourage this. Nothing prevents the state regulator from drawing a "red line" or a border between "right" and "wrong" wherever, from their point of view, it is sorely needed.

The first thing I realized when studying economics was that nothing is free. And measures to establish order are no exception. Costs also need to be justified and some measurable impact delivered. The loss of those who one day ventured beyond the "red line," from the category of law-abiding citizen to that of criminal, is not taken into account by the System. But from the point of view of the GDP, which, with the help of the System, we are unsuccessfully attempting to raise, this is a gross loss. To save the business, the offender has to pass costs onto customers. Should they fail and go bankrupt, it'll turn out to have even more of an impact on all the underdog's partners and our bottom line.

One time, in St. Petersburg, everyone found out about the existence of a "skyline," set at a height of forty meters, along which all planned and in-progress construction projects had to be leveled, from the city center to its very borders. That was a new vision of the local governor and the head of the architecture committee. Building height restrictions had been adopted immediately, without allowing anyone to finish projects that had already been agreed upon and started, even on the outskirts and in residential areas where this "line" had not been visible for a long time. The issue was most likely so important that it would brook no delay and the System decided to ignore developers' losses. Though a proviso was added stipulating opportunities to toil away for "extra" floors on a case-by-case basis.

It's not just "extra" floors that might fall beyond the red line. For example, the next time when the System became interested in the promotion of homemade surrogates of foreign mediations because it interfered with the harmonization of the foreign exchange balance, the red line was easily moved, and all "inconvenient" pills were declared as restricted. What could be more important than order? And the regulator really is trying very hard, orienting itself primarily by ear, by the volume of the squeak of those being crushed by the new version of the rules.

The System discovers it can designate almost anyone as a half-guilty offender. Furthermore, one need not punish the actual violator; it's enough to find someone who resembles them by and large and who, at the same time, won't object too loudly. Rules and classifiers that encourage fast-and-loose interpretations leave open the opportunity to, at best, negotiate the size of the penalty. It takes perseverance and endurance to prove the System wrong.

Everything seems relatively clear in the customs code. For example, importers are charged a duty rate consisting of a percentage of the customs value. Fiddling with this value, overestimating or underestimating it, makes sense only if somewhere farther down the chain there's a break, like a criminal operation that allows you to "clean and remove" the difference. Otherwise, the tax department collects what you tried to hide from customs anyway. In our case, custom writes its own instructions on how to recognize a potential swindler belonging to a certain "risk group" in order to charge as much as it deems appropriate.

No one is perplexed when the head of the customs department announces a list of who among the large importers are obliged to agree with the prices on imported goods that customs consider correct. Those in disagreement will simply be served with as many problems as possible. According to the same code, however, we must rely on the actual prices by which further bookkeeping is conducted. All this is taken for granted. The majority is just trying to negotiate and bargain for more favorable conditions. It's no surprise when, in a couple of years, the customs department boss himself ends up playing the starring role in another corruption scandal. The situation is painfully familiar to those who had those long conversations "by the code" in the '90s, and who might have ended up ensnared by a strange logic according to which, by definition, they owed something.

My company imported construction materials from the European Union and, of course, immediately fell into the "risk group" because, according to the logic of the customs inspector, it was 100 percent a half-guilty offender (that is, crooked). For several years, we were offered one after another "elastic" option, what papers to fill out and who to give them to, to do everything "like everybody does." They convinced me that agreeing we were a little bit like a half-guilty offender wouldn't hurt at all and wasn't even that expensive.

The problem wasn't our adherence to principles. We just had to submit financial statements to the foreign shareholders and explain everything. We were assisted by the need to answer a timely and well-formulated question. The controller from Germany could not for the life of them understand why it was necessary either to distort or replace the real invoice (the slip for the delivered goods) in order to pass through the customs procedure. I tried to explain until I caught myself feeling like I was becoming, in the eyes of my colleagues, something like a character from the planet Tatooine in *Star Wars* with a proboscis, little wings, and very dubious motivations. All that remained was to throw in the towel and file for customs in the arbitrations court.

There was little to recommend this choice. For several years, we were a "black sheep," constantly overpaying due to our intractability (or, in more direct terms, "for being so stupid"). On the other hand, it was easier to report to people who didn't understand any formulation of the question besides the correct one. Gradually, we accumulated volume, and we ourselves became a large part of the very statistics into which the customs inspector had tried to rush us. We went through cassations and appeals, and, a couple years later, we were given back the payments charged to us for "looking guilty" according to a combination of formal features. Or, more precisely, what was left of them after the hike in inflation.

Now for another story about skipping physics lessons. Remember how, in previous chapters, we found calculations and supporting evidence too mundane and swapped them out for formal procedures based on the principle of "the regulator isn't opposed"? Especially if we're talking about some kind of sewer pipe in a small Siberian town that, according to project specs, had to be built from cast iron. The contractor offered to build it from cheaper plastic, agreed on the change with everyone who had to agree, built it, handed it over, and got paid.

A few years later, he messed with someone on a more serious project. When they came to his house with a search warrant and took him to the pre-trial detention center, he learned a lot about himself by reading investigation documents. The truth, as the System sees it, was revealed according to the prosecution: Cast iron, which has a service life of no less than a whole century, was switched out for plastic, which can only be considered reliable for up to fifty years. Therefore, the builder cheated everyone, and for that, he had to suffer a well-deserved punishment along with everyone else who agreed to the change. Yet again, because of such an opinion, which there was no one around to challenge, and suitable words in the documentation, written either by someone unsportsmanlike or poorly educated, were found as justification.

I have already mentioned that since the first half of the 20th century, the determination of service life has been part of the puzzle in physics. Even cast iron can be broken quickly by exceeding its permissible load or rendered unusable after a couple of years by running the discharge of some kind of chemical production through it. If you calculate the reliability of urban sewer networks, then a service life of fifty years is normative and reasonable. Experience shows that a lot can change over such a period, and, therefore, it's easier and cheaper to build new networks than to design something eternal. This is if they do the calculations and comprehend the task on, at the very least, a high school level.

As far as the calculation of reliability and service life to be an empty formality and yet, now a prosecutor, in a studied voice, affecting memorized accents, spews complete nonsense from the point of view of a technically competent person. Cast iron with a 100-year service life was firmly entrenched in the minds of those who wrote the indictment. The judge listened, nodded, and sent the defendants back to the prison cell for another couple of months. The enterprise was unraveling, dozens of employees were scattering to the winds, and equipment was being sold off for a pittance... They offered the contractor a chance to acquiesce, to concede to the absurdity of the nonsensical reasoning heaped before him, to not resist in vain, and to slip into the berth of "guilty" that had been prepared just for him.

The representative of the System slots the simple and familiar words into the formulas they need and reads them as they like. All that is left is to agree with these mantras in order to take in this nightmare that's suddenly materialized.

The System begins to identify threats and their sources, fighting them with all the power of its own imagination. Retail outlets at busy spots in our megacities that had been constructed several years ago in accordance with all local regulations suddenly start climbing onto underground communications lines (or did the comm lines themselves suddenly climb beneath them?). Next round, these pavilions are also ugly, inconsistent, and not uniform, spoiling the landscape, historical appearance, and the mood of townspeople with a heightened sense of beauty. Lastly, our System suggests that the booths of street vendors occupy a key place in the plans of possible terrorists. Just yesterday, authorities defined that danger may come from any outlet located closer than fifty meters to the metro station; now, that threat radius has grown to 100. Who can explain such a direct logical correlation from the terrorist to the hot dog stand and on what model of infernal machine is this effect radius based? But if you ask a lot of questions, then the safety distance might easily expand to 200 meters. Nobody cares about the sacrifice of real values for the sake of imagined order. Somebody lost his job or property, and another one wasted extra time getting his snack or cup of coffee away from his usual route.

It took two years to issue a judgment on the hostel, for example, which offended neighbors are unhappy with, and the legislator is obliged to protect them at the cost of destroying the hostel itself. If we define the threat directly, then it would be dirt, noise, and a criminal milieu, the diseases of any large gathering of poorly organized and ill-mannered people. In this scenario, the problem can be identified, and localized, and a resolution attempted. But where is the direct, unconditional connection with the sign that says "hostel"? Removal of the "hostel" will not result in a decrease in unwanted guests. Those same people—the sources of problems, dirt, and noise—will not disappear from the city. They'll just disperse throughout dormitories and rented apartments, where they'll go on to bother new neighbors. Someone will be out of a means of earning money, and somebody else will lose their safe and affordable accommodation.

The System just needs a good excuse to get excited. It seems like finding and punishing the guilty is what gets it going. Manufacturers complain that retailers are returning expired products to them. But the manufacturer is our sacred cow, and the System rushes to their defense. Now, owners of retail spaces will bear the costs, but the customer, for whom all this hullabaloo is just a fuss about shifting money from pocket to pocket, will end up paying for everything. It's just economic and all expenses of the seller are to be covered by the buyer, or the seller becomes bankrupt. The management companies providing utility services are checked, fined, and can be changed multiple times in a year. Only the money for all the fines and reorganizations comes out of the pockets of those who complain about the provided service. Moreover, the problem itself and the threat will, as a result, remain exactly as they are. It's worth looking at the situation a bit more broadly and remembering that nothing is free, and, in the final tally, everyone pays for maintaining order. The goal is to minimize losses—achievable if antagonists work towards that together, without rushing to appeal to the System.

The Prosecutor's Office and Investigative Committee are the final authority and practically obligatory participants in all disputes, including child development, architecture, medicine, morality, theatre problems, and higher education. The System is energetically activated if it is necessary to serve justice in the relationship between employee and employer, or to force people to be more respectful towards some sacred thing.

The result is always the same. Regulators and controllers will cheerfully report on successes in cost savings, impeccably performed rituals and procedures, that everything has now been named and counted "as it should be," that the guilty have been punished, and that now everything is "in compliance." The System will help, support, and save its denizens from threats, despite the fact that the main source of risk and generator of losses has long been the System itself.

The "blood drinkers" have created for themselves an unlimited field of action. They have set themselves a goal, vital and almost achievable, like chasing their own tail. The guilty will always be in abundance and can be collected at will, like hunting for mushrooms in the woods. In the zero-sum game, the search for the weakest link in the food chain has become a regularity. There's another side effect of the endless restoration of order that only delays opportunities to set the situation right—the bloat of Big Everything.

~ CHAPTER NINE ~
BIG BODY

A representative of the category calling itself "people of the sovereign," responsible for water transport safety, once gave a precise and unexpected formulation of our specific method of management. As it turns out, the country still doesn't operate according to codified laws but by case law, just in a special interpretation. He told me: "If there's a precedent, there's a problem. A precedent is when it's loud or there are victims. Then we'll deal with it to the fullest extent. And if there's no precedent making a big noise, then there's no problem."

In other words, there's no set task for managing the probability of error. It's enough to just react to the precedent itself, punishing the perpetrators if possible, carrying out demonstrative measures to strengthen control, and then waiting for the next one. The System can break up and interpret this task as it sees fit, shifting losses to its subjects and its partners in a once-favorable compromise. The System remains unteachable and will never lack for the punished or the guilty on whom will fall the costs of restoring order. Unteachable, because that's unprofitable for the System itself so long as its responsibility for the implementation of the overall task remains nominal.

Ideally, the size and shape of the governing structure are linked to the task we're attempting to do. In simpler cases, when it's possible to articulate comprehensible general rules, participants can get along on their own. For more complex endeavors, networks with local, independent command centers must be established; and the most complex, large-scale, and riskiest tasks call for the creation of hierarchical pyramids governing all those involved. So long as a connection to the common goal is preserved, we retain the ability to apply any and all known methods of optimization and improvements in management efficiency.

We have created a situation in which either government regulation is in effect, or nothing is. There are neither simple nor complex tasks, universal nor specific. The state is endowed with power and capabilities, and interprets and changes all these tasks for itself, resolving them as best it can. No one is making any effort to counterbalance its heavy argumentation. Then, under the pretense of establishing order, the System takes its cut from those who can't figure it out on their own, who can't even imagine that there might be another means for creating order that doesn't call for the participation of a person in uniform. The System representatives explain it as establishing and maintaining order, but I hardly believe that they know what this order looks like in detail.

The practical question is the maintenance of a house under collective ownership. At a minimum, it must be kept in working order and not allowed to fall into disrepair. At a maximum, the owners ought to invest in their property. After all, the market value of any dwelling, if it needs to be mortgaged or sold, is dependent on the condition of the pipes, roof, and stairs.

A decision must be reached that suits all the owners. Then a plan must be drawn up, materials must be found, and a worker needed to complete the project. Someone must act on behalf of the collective client, collecting or borrowing money, selecting contractors, and reporting on progress. If we approach the task rationally, then its resolution will call for a certain number of workers—relatively speaking, ten people employed on the project for a conditional two hundred labor hours. In a well-organized market, the cost of the whole set can be determined with an accuracy of between 10 to 20 percent. In a poorly organized one, price dispersion and risk can increase indefinitely.

According to my experience, the task might become impossible after the first question is asked: "What do I need this for...?" The whole saga of collecting money, explaining there was no backroom dealing, and that nobody stole anything is a whole other drama. The task of a separate house will be passed to the highest level of the federal state machine. Repairs will become unavoidable, and in this manner, they may be pushed back for eternity. A conditional, mid-tier house must be invented for a representative city, or, perhaps, for a district, or, even better, for the whole country at once. Then we can figure out how to fix this virtual house and how much that would cost. Laws and regulations must also be composed and adopted, and a governing structure created at the federal level. Lastly, money must be collected from everyone, and seventy billion rubles might be accumulated during the first year before it's determined what to do with them. For each house, thousands of different people will spend a few seconds at the level of a federal ministry or several hours at the level of an urban area, and nobody will be doing anything for free.

The ultimate source of financing will not change. It's the pockets of those same owners. In addition to direct repair costs, they'll shell out extra on account of being unable to agree on a budget, aesthetics, and the answer to the question of who needs this. You can call it an infantilism tax. It's paid by everyone who finds consolation in the fact that they didn't take responsibility for themselves and didn't allow their neighbor to get away with being clever.

The interference of a regulator is justified when it decreases transaction costs, minimizes risks for economic subjects, and paves the way for fair competition. Considering the above, the System is not able to fulfill this function anymore. Such a situation is unavoidable when any kind of basic logic is blurred by compromises and so many Mimics involved in the management process. The planning and implementation of these plans also give some curious results. We designed and supplied water tanks for installation high in the mountains as a part of the preparation for the Olympic Games in Sochi 2014. In one, I discovered a huge, reinforced concrete wall around my tanks that appeared in the project design. It made no sense in terms of any technical issues and caused nothing but delays and troubles. I asked my contractor: "What is the function of this wall? What kind of loads is it suggested to bear?"

He thought for a while and then he said: "Money."

Then he sighed and added: "A lot of money."

As a first step, the System with control and power but without defined actual goals acquires a feature of a tumor that just slows a common dynamic, but also a "taste for blood" or plain biological hunger makes this tumor rather malignant than useless.

Somewhere in Austria, Sri Lanka, and even Uganda, the construction of a small hydroelectric power plant on a river is a task feasibly undertaken by a single municipality and a private contractor. But in Russia, it's only a subject for many years of discussion and the formation of state programs. As well, we regulate the collection of waste and garbage in such a way that few people will risk investment in full-fledged industrial processing without having secured agreements with the System and guarantees at the highest possible level. If there's no more space around the metropolis, then the garbage will simply shift to where there is space. The direction depends on the winds—which way will they blow and who else will start choking on the stench and blocking federal highways? Another mega-task arises, which our good friends—those who call everything by the "right" names and manipulate data—will resolve with a deafening drumbeat and unwavering success.

Now, the state is developing a federal program with billions in budgetary support and the obligatory participation of an unsinkable innovator on a national scale for the majority of these tasks. Private contractors are hardly able to secure approvals for any big project, and these deals may not even last long. All it takes is to change or rearrange one significant authority, and any plans start unraveling, because the new Big Boss brings a new control team and can give a new interpretation to local codes and rules.

Since 2009, approval of the President has become obligatory for all candidates for the local governorship in Russia. Actually, he has the right to appoint them. First of all, new authorities revised all significant cash flows and big investment projects. Many of them had been frozen or canceled under the pretense "to improve an order." New power launches other projects, which they declare more important than those initiated by predecessors. It caused a wave of bankruptcies of contractors and waste of already made investments, which nobody tried to analyze and claim. Then we lost one and a half million dollars on one construction site in Moscow, but the point is that the whole project worth more than 40 million dollars and completed for 90 percent remains useless more than ten years since this campaign "in the name of order."

The regulator can find an "incorrect" process or "almost ownerless" flow of money anywhere. Where one does not yet exist, any hungry representative of the System will find there a subject for conversation, reserving the last word for itself. Areas appear in which there are no comprehensible conditions from the primary and singular regulator, and they can, at any moment, go to "restore order," should they feel the urge. They can similarly rewrite these conditions as they please to restore order anew.

The System grows and concentrates resources and power, but its actual governability degrades. Any one of the System's control processes can lead to a dead end or fall into a protective stupor if there arises any doubt about the "correctness" of what is happening. It's enough for the System to act according to its instructions and make the safest of all possible decisions—that is, to do nothing. The System no longer stumbles across anyone's clearly expressed readiness to solve things on their own, independently. It's the only organized structure and it can only be guided by the need to maintain its stability, appetite, and the possibilities of its "food supply." So, what about its physiology? The System begins to grow like a Big Body, taking up all available space. In conjunction with the Big Body, symbiotic commercial organizations can be created that operate with a high mandate and full support. They will weigh, count, control, digitize, label, track, and charge for it. It's just that now most of the acquired funds will go to feed the symbiote itself. The leftovers go to the originally declared goal.

In this situation, the only reliable and singularly correct place for money is the state budget and all the financial institutions that fall under the complete control of the Big Body. Funneling money into these bottomless pockets under the pretext of maintaining order and then using these funds in the singularly correct way shouldn't inspire any doubts. Everything that goes there is correctly placed and almost never discussed. That which gets passed by is at the very least suspicious and subject to verification.

Everything that happens in the economy falls into direct and critical dependence on the consuming, digesting, and redistributing processes taking place inside the Big Body. There, a portion of the funds will settle, a portion will dissolve, and the remainder will be spent in the established, agreed-upon, and correct manner.

Plans are written for each task and a centralized set of control structures is created. Taking these plans in their initial state as feasible can be a very big stretch. Mega-projects start out as fun, but they can easily skid to a halt in the middle of the road. Workers—those who "couldn't cut it"—are again wasted. The project ends up being completed by those who came in third or fourth, and the latter are sometimes lured by deceit or even coerced via blackmail. Those who directly design, manufacture, build, and process are pushed further and further to the edge, where they join the ranks of the "lost." The "Invincibles" of the governing structures remain in place, but there isn't anyone left to fulfill their plans. When, finally, a budget is allocated for a specific task and the project reaches the implementation stage, then workers need to be found. The task is to find "somebody" who will do everything for the money left over after all the verifications, "optimizations," and expensive management rituals. But this "somebody" never materializes—they've disappeared, died out, or left the job in their specialty a long time ago.

The Big Body begins to consume everything like a black hole. This is the largest receptacle of funds collected under the premise of "providing benefit to all," solving all problems at once instead of concrete and achievable ones. It won't turn out well. And there's never enough money. Big Body declares to solve all problems for everyone, describing in general terms how it plans to handle these issues. Nobody can argue or balance Big Body's hunger because there is no alternative, sustainable option of control.

There is no one Big Body that can collect so much and distribute it in such a way that will leave everyone full and satisfied. That's because, in this formulation, not a single money problem has a solution. This is a retelling of the story in which several people are sharing one pie and every single one is certain that half of it belongs to them. One thinks this because they brought all the flour; the second, because their oven was used to bake it; the third brought the most important ingredient—raisins;

but the one with the sharp knife in their hand, with which they'll cut both the pie and carelessly outstretched fingers, will take the most.

The growing size and complexity of the structure of the Big Body are hardly connected with certain and correctly defined management goals. It's rather physiological and it's just a matter of time—when different parts of the Big Body start to bite each other. The pie that they try to share becomes smaller because of the loss of common efficiency but there is more than one participant with the sharp knife at the table. Various power structures of "order keepers" inevitably conflict with each other provoking new corruption scandals. The result is negative anyway because such a System is not learning, and its main operation logic stays the same. The sacrifice of compromised contractors and their counterparts in the state structure became a useless distraction and a reason for new economic losses.

Benefits go to those who pretend to control the Big Body and several who succeeded with adaptation. Overall losses slowing down are hardly manageable. The System becomes very stable as far as it is hardly movable now. It can be successful and eternal in isolation, but it is losing in competition with other versions of the System that retain the ability to change and optimize.

The most heated and continuous discussion, however, is being held on this score: What should be done with the Big Body into which our System has devolved, and how best to manage its capabilities? A very popular version is that the Big Body, which concentrates most of the available resources, is the basis of an upcoming Big Breakthrough.

~ CHAPTER TEN ~
THE BIG BREAKTHROUGH

As you can imagine, I'm one of those people who begins thinking through a problem only when I've thoroughly banged my head against it. In short, I'm not a wise man, and I'm not particularly fortunate. But after another setback at the end of the '90s, the idea of going to university for a degree in economics turned out to be not so bad. If your own mind doesn't have enough knowledge, it makes sense to look for it in others. It's even better when you can add your own thoughts to what you've learned. Moreover, I was lucky enough to fall flat on my face with appendicitis in the hospital three days before a defense of my graduate work. They wouldn't allow me to reschedule, and proposed, as an alternative, that I come back next year. After the abdominal operation, my stomach swelled up and it became very uncomfortable. Painkillers and sleeping pills did nothing to pep me up. But skulking away with my tail between my legs, one step before the finish line, was even more revolting. Hiding my stomach and unbuttoned trousers under my jacket, quietly, sideways, I came and sat down before the committee empty-handed. An examiner who'd been invited from another university thought I was being impudent and sicced himself on me like a terrier. Defending what I myself had understood, thought, and written about turned out not to be at all difficult, but soon I asked him to wrap things up. The professor had just taken a breath, preparing to work himself into a fit and rip me to shreds, when I confessed that I was about ready to pass out into a dead faint in the most shameful of ways.

Here's another saying for you from one of my German colleagues: *"Unkrautvergehtnicht."* Something about bad weeds you'll never be able to pull out completely. And for me, this can be said about the sort of thought that pulls you forward when all hope is lost. And you don't even have to believe strongly, so long as you know exactly what you're doing.

From 2008 to 2009, things got all shaken up again when we got the impact of the worldwide economic crisis—but I turned out to have been better prepared that time. Evidently, I did learn something at university. But then 2015 came along with a new crisis provoked by Russian interference in Ukrainian affairs. Again, prospects were so-so, and, according to all the textbooks, the opinions of colleagues, and advice "as seen on TV," it was time to throw in the towel—there were no tips, no hopes...

I had to look for a new idea.

But where to go looking? Best of all, in the economic forum of our most important metropolitan university, at which the most distinguished speakers were gathered.

There, I heard something like this...

According to presenters in the course of the experiments called "liberalization," we forgot that the Russian mentality, generally speaking, is entirely different, and our path is unique! Furthermore, over there they have crisis after crisis, while we, as it turns out, had seventy whole years of steady development, victory, and success. We have lost our power, our confidence, our strategic advantages. We must regain what was lost, act as a united front, concentrate, accumulate, and direct... These magical mantras brought the speakers and the audience into such ecstasy and inspired such confidence that it seemed as though we would immediately burst forth from the rut, rushing out, taking off, and moving onto a lofty trajectory as soon as we exited the auditorium. All that was needed was to bring the ideas to the very top of the chain, come to an agreement, draft and approve the documents, and imbue them with the highest possible status.

The greatest confidence is inspired by the Great Plans peddled by the most authoritative of people. They convincingly demonstrate that our future success depends only on the volume of the Big Body's pocket, and on how successfully and correctly its contents will be invested. Meanwhile, we'll mobilize and concentrate, generate and discuss strategies. The main thing is not getting bogged down in details so as not to lose inspiration.

Am I the only one who thinks that if a plan includes abstract concepts like the appearance of eureka moments, raw talent, extraordinary discoveries, feats, and anything else that falls into the category of "miraculous," it's just a really bad plan? To put it bluntly, it's an absolutely lousy plan, and the drafters of such a plan would be better off trying to find self-actualization in some other field.

Once again, we'll make sacrifices in the name of something understood by the chosen few now receiving applause, nodding and smiling as they watch their recipes for success "soak in." We'll get a feat; we'll drive ourselves into this familiar mode. Meanwhile, the distance from the eureka moment to the result becomes like that separating da Vinci's drafts from Igor Sikorsky's blueprints. The genius of the Renaissance made impressive pictures of flying devices but none of them were able to take off, in contrast to the creations of the pioneer of helicopter engineering.

Again, we're searching for answers at the very top of our System. I won't be mistaken if I say that everything is based on the supposition that the top posts are occupied by people who really know how best to use available resources and the possibilities of the present situation. At least, that's what they're trying to tell us.

We'll leave the intricacies of the state apparatus alone for now. Let's turn to something understandable—the economy. We will proceed from the assumption that, independent of the rank of the position occupied, it is held, all the same, by a person who is, therefore, unable to go beyond human capabilities, no matter how much we might desire it. The expectation that a brilliant insight will certainly come to this person after they've been given an appointment, empowered, and dressed in a suit is what I would call "overly optimistic." It is, of course, difficult to find the necessary number of geniuses, and those who are not "geniuses" (instead, our old friends, the masters of mimicry) behave as they always do: They gather together other people's known and proven solutions and write off readymade answers that, from their point of view, will make an impression on their most important customers.

The hope that everything will work out for them, the confidence that the guarantee of our "tomorrow" is a Big Bag filled to bursting, keeps people in hand just as well as violence and faith.

A small addition from the Big Body or regulatory preferences may turn out to be enough to make the choice of the state representative decisive, as had been in the planned economy. The actual buyer will not decide what they need from the array offered by the actual seller; rather, they'll each receive what the System selects for them. Instead of the dimwitted "market," capable only of spoiling everything, and instead of end buyers, the choice will be made by a group of people who can see twenty years into the future, with encyclopedic knowledge, unimpeachable honesty and integrity and, most importantly, who still have to agree among themselves. Next comes the competition among potential champions, not, in actuality, a competition of projects or products, but a fight for a handout for support from the Big Body. The System makes its decision, using a large scale, and selects an "innovative cluster" or "economic driver," guided by some shared traits.

It's hard to miss that these strategies are usually based on the ideas of others. More often than not, what's proposed is something that's already been done abroad. Then there are the veiled attempts to follow in the footsteps of yesterday's leaders, all while pretending we're about to outpace everyone. A rather paradoxical approach, I must say.

The chances of any new product depend on the number of people who might need it and, on their ability, to pay for it (i.e., on their knack for exchanging labor time and knowledge for money). Success depends on the speed of the road from inventor to buyer, on the number of roadblocks and checkpoints at which the potential of this novelty must be assessed by outsiders, nonetheless very important people. These assessors take money and choices from silly customers too foolish to make decisions for themselves.

For example, a Finnish man who drew an angry, fluffy bird and combined his slingshot skills with the capabilities of a touchpad—could he count on the Big Break? Would ministers and academics have guessed that this simple app called Angry

ASKING THE RIGHT QUESTIONS

Birds would wind up being worth a billion?

At one of those conferences for the promotion of composite materials, a speaker kept repeating the refrain: Our product is better than the rest because it's "the most high-tech, innovative..." and other popular adjectives. Somewhere along the way, the right questions got lost. What was their product "better than"? In what scenarios? Why? At that same conference, a representative of the state monopoly responsible for the development and fostering of innovation lamented to the audience: Why is it that the innovative products in question begin showing cracks and fall apart in the first five years out of the promised hundred? Well, sure, the strength of materials theory is still stronger than Russian legislation, but does that really matter when we're talking about the Big Breakthrough?

The real utility of "innovation" could be sorted out by specialists. For starters, they could read the documentation and determine what is lacking in order to produce a full-fledged product with the desired characteristics. Then, these same professionals could think about how the novelty might be productively used to solve specific problems and seriously expect an overall positive effect. Instead, most of the discussion concerned how to pitch the fruits of your creativity as some kind of ideal product that is "better than all the rest," by definition, directly to the president. If you can't get the president, then how do you convey your innovative ideas to the relevant ministers, at the very least? It is they who must "appraise," "help," and "support" to move innovation forward.

It seems that they did "appraise" and "support," as a "development strategy" was adopted under which a sum of three billion rubles (about 50 million US dollars, a pittance for the Big Body) was promised for distribution within potential partners. At the moment these funds were allocated, they expected to launch within ten years "new high-tech, innovative" products with a total output of at least a hundred billion a year. Five years passed, and a small part of the funds was already being distributed little by little to those who seemed like future champions, judging by a set of formal features. To be on the safe side, it was worth adding a couple of templates from an MBA course littered with jargon, playing around with some statistics, drawing some steadily growing graphs, and all other favorite skills of Mimics. As with the "secret of the goat," a deep understanding and detailed evidence aren't necessary. The main thing is to use vivid images and generalizations, act like we're on the cutting edge, or just about to be, and avoid certain obligations.

A fair share of the money allocated goes to the same conferences, presentations, and seminars. Another portion is spent on absurd marketing research to find and promote the product that, by definition, is simply "the best." The "innovative breakthrough" product doesn't see its own niche or the substitute products that haven't yet been appended with such broad definitions.

At this conference, an elderly aircraft designer was presenting and, in response to one too many insistent calls to introduce fashionable composites, he lost his cool and yelled: "Leave my machine alone!" He just wasn't interested in seeking out politically correct maneuvers. He had, rather, built his own plane, which ought to fly.

Another aspect of the miracle built into the "domestic" breakthrough plan is to raid the pockets of your customers in exchange for a promise to be just about to overtake external competitors who possess an order of magnitude, if not two, more production and capabilities. The resulting champion remains one only in greenhouse conditions, where they can rewrite the rules themselves and buyers have been deprived of choice. Said champion is immediately blown out of the water when having to compete on an equal footing. And they'll have to compete. That's the only way to increase volumes by an order of magnitude, and make use of economies of scale, opportunities for cooperation, and division of labor.

Nobody is arguing against support for priority projects. In fact, practically everyone does it, and Japanese Zaibatsu and Korean Chaebol can be cited as examples. But it's just a tool, and as such, everything depends on who is using it and how. When the Big Body outweighs all other economic agents and the most important customer is the state itself, then the effect can be completely adverse. There will be fuss and a lot of words, expenditures on measures for the support of grandiose programs, but there won't be any growth or clear results. No one will remember the burst bubbles of "strategies" and "development programs" after a few years. That is, unless they see value in the ability of individuals to spout off a lot of well-placed buzzwords, they establish a dizzying career as successful managers. Flashy presentations describe the flock of cargo airships flying, the hi-tech glasses with artificial intelligence that purchase their owner a tie of their own accord, inspiring our specialists with strategic innovations... It makes an impression one doesn't soon forget. Is it the result of powerful meditation, or did they just smoke too much?

Excessive interference by the Big Body has another negative general effect: Horizons and planning opportunities shrink for all private economic subjects. The first thing the designated "champion" does is trample down those who lost the race for support from the Big Body, as well as anyone else who is smaller. This is how the dairy herd in large holdings will grow, receiving preferential treatment and subsidies, while, at the same time, the total number of livestock will remain the same due to the extinction of small farms.

The Big Body doesn't generate money to feed the "future champion"; that money is collected from "everyone else" whose interests the System has deemed less important. The venture will prove justified when this champion actually produces a better product for cheaper and delivers returns on the advances given. It's assumed that one day, the champions themselves will stop receiving "strategic" preference, and along with the regulator will correct all the lies in the documentation, resurrect their smaller competitors, and lower prices... But before that, the System will shift money from others' "incorrect" pockets into just one, the "most correct."

Not only does the Big Body's money get parsed out unfairly, but the System finds ways to further fill its coffers, feeding new "symbiotes" that collect money from across the country for "breakthroughs" or "establishing order." It furthermore turns out that the whole point is that our economic processes are "under-digitized." It's quite necessary to digitize everything and then we'll definitely surpass everyone abroad. For some reason, however, our competitors were managing well with many things even before the invention of barcodes and broadband Internet. Integers only are helpful if they're plugged into a correctly written algorithm. It's a tool in the hands of a person who understands the actual process and can describe it with the help of a program.

So long as we're "just a little" confused about our specifications and our agricultural complexes are not able to provide products in the required volumes without resorting to tons of palm oil, a barcode won't help. On the contrary, it'll most certainly increase overall expenses and, in conjunction with complicated licensing procedures, will become an additional barrier to small businesses.

When drafting large-scale initiatives, big and costly projects for the "creation of growth infrastructure" look good. You can build bridges and roads and evaluate them based on investment costs without really thinking about who's going to use them. A more modern version of this is to choose a territory and direct resources there, creating greenhouse conditions, and then waiting for the Big Breakthrough: The arrival of investors, the appearance of brilliant ideas and geniuses, something comparable in scale to the first spaceflight of Yuri Gagarin in 1961.

So, the "*Moglino* Special Economic Zone," a project worth three billion two hundred million rubles (again, about 50 million US dollars), was unveiled with a great deal of pomp in 2016. Five years after the grand opening, it's still a beautiful fence hung with cameras, behind which there are more than 200 hectares of land crisscrossed by roads lined with lights and all communications lines laid down. In the corners are several buildings. In one, dried snacks are packaged; in the other, varnishes and paints. The rest is a plantation of top-quality hogweed. Behind the fence, there's also some cow parsnip. In the rankings of similar "priority development zones," this project once came seventh out of fifteen. Another billion-dollar question: What does the "priority development" look like in the eight that rated lower?

All these are shells that only acquire real value to the extent that they are inhabited. As it turns out, however, there is nothing with which to fill them as far as the whole economy outside is exhausted by Big Body itself and the negative processes mentioned above. Something ends up working out, if only because a lot of resources have been expended. These successes are achieved according to the favorite formula of supporters of concentration and mobilization: "At any cost." This formula is so loved by those who do not have to pay the price themselves and who forget to specify how the benefits of these great achievements will be shared by all. First, we assume we'll create champions, then later we'll think about how and by what principle they'll share with those who remained outside the plans for the big economic breakthrough, if these bottle-fed leaders will share anything at all. The overwhelming majority don't participate in breakthroughs or invent anything new. They're not geniuses or drivers; for the most part, people do familiar, understandable things and work that isn't terribly difficult. These are the same buyers who must ensure the final demand for the fruits of the "breakthroughs" and genius discoveries. If they can't manage this task, then no number of brilliant ideas and growth strategies will help.

Once we understand the Big Body isn't everything and that its enhancement comes at the cost of depleting the limited resources of the rest of the "disordered" economy, then hopes for the Big Breakthrough start to fade. The System ignores its own mistakes. We lose because we're less organized. Our System doesn't work towards common goals. Mostly, it works for itself. It's not a ladder you can use to climb higher, but a swamp where the more you struggle, the faster you drown. No, we can still become champions if everyone else agrees to play like we do in the dark of night, barefoot and a little drunk.

There is another option for solving all the problems and achieving success in the economy, no less popular and convincing enough at first glance.

Let's change the System, or, even better, break it down and build it up again from scratch…

~ CHAPTER ELEVEN ~
CHANGE FOR CHANGE'S SAKE

Okay, let's go hunting for clues again. This time those who argue with the System and blame it for all our failures.

I went to a meeting where the System's critics gathered. At first glance, everything was clear: We had to follow the example of states with more successful economies than ours. Everything seemed simple: The most effective institutions and highest levels of development are found in countries with democratic systems. There was no doubt that these countries are doing well because their leaders are replaced regularly, and electoral procedures are carried out more or less flawlessly. An exception does need to be made in the cases of South Korea or China, where economic development has also proceeded fairly well under the most authoritarian and irremovable leaders. One speaker—by some strange coincidence, a professional financier—expressed the seditious sentiment that democracy in and of itself does not guarantee economic success.

Such a statement was not popular with the excited audience. Even the most radical zealot with an unkempt beard suggested the doubter be ostracized and never invited back. The discussion was hushed up. And to think—it was just putting some meat on its bones, making arguments more logical and less emotional.

At that same meeting, some very serious people proposed solving the problems with justice quite simply by following the example of Singapore and appealing to the High Court of London for help. The logic was ironclad: Did the Court of London help Singapore? It helped. Was there an economic miracle and a victory over corruption in Singapore? There was. Therefore, we should just do as "everyone else" did. The fact that the state system of Singapore was built by the British for almost one hundred years prior to its independence and that Singapore and Russia are, to put it mildly, countries of varying complexity and incomparable scale are details that now fall on deaf ears. Furthermore, no one asked the High Court of London if it needed the case.

The most outspoken critics of the System focus on state hierarchy. They are certain that everything will turn out better faster if one or more figures at the very top are changed. Some are more inspired by the word *overthrow*. They are protesting against something, of course, but it's not always clear does they have an understandable alternative or something better than abstract ideas. Moreover, thirty years ago (which is quite recent, by the standards of history), we already broke and changed a System. We even had shots fired from tanks in the center of the capital. These changes didn't come cheaply at all, in case anyone's forgotten, and the results have left many disappointed.

The accusers blame the general audience for not listening to them and not responding. But they can't bring anything new to the table, just the already familiar abstract constructions and habitual attacks on the System. People are no longer prepared to rush forward, because they did it already, following common feelings without an actual plan.

The bumbling reaction of the System to criticism keeps you from getting bored and once more tosses out some good excuses. The Big Body and its symbiotes are just as concerned about their health as those who don't like them very much are concerned about their own. According to them, the System is in a constant state of optimization and renewal, and modernizers within the System spout off just about the same words as the critics outside of it. They're just trying to correct mistakes, not to understand how and why the mistakes were made. No one admits their real blunders or analyzes them, and, in the course of correction, with no less zeal, makes new ones.

I came across a multipage file from 2016 by the Center for Strategic Research called "Analysis of Factors in the Implementation of Top-Level Strategic Planning Documents." In it, I read proposals on how to eliminate excessive regulation in the construction industry. And I came across a proposition to remove from practice the only thing that ought to remain: calculations and supporting evidence. Modernizers write them off as "redundant" quite easily. In the same file, there was another in-depth analysis that made quite an impression on me. As the basis of the analysis, the author looked at the frequency with which key phrases were mentioned in the text of new documents. "Institutions" and "institutional" were brought up more than 200 times, meaning that they're being modernized, and so everything will be fine. The editor of this text found only three references to the judicial and law enforcement systems, meaning that everything with modernization in those fields is going poorly.

So, yes, the System operates clumsily. But what does replacing the figures at the very top produce in itself? The question isn't what the name of the leader is and when we replace them, but whether or not they can work out the System's kinks. To have any economic effect, liberalization and the triumph of democracy must correct obvious errors in the management of economic processes. If we go by things that are said during election campaigns, all those promises to sort everything out and fix it, then everything ought to turn out fine. But if, besides vague words and other people's examples, there isn't even a working schema, then, in all likelihood, the chosen character will end up doing much the same: inspire, be a figurehead, and sow seeds of hope that everything will be on the up-and-up... and so on, until the next election!

It's probably worth starting from the fact that any method of construction for a System can only be considered good if it works; that is, if it allows the System to generate solutions in a timely manner. If the collective, democratic discussion of such decisions doesn't produce such solutions, then is there really such an undeniable and almost sacred meaning to it? If we're talking about the successes of the authoritarian regimes in Southeast Asia—where the System doesn't bother trying to circumvent laws that no one really can—then there's every chance of success when racing forth from "humble beginnings." Later on, however, the authoritarian leader must face the growing complexity of the developing system, and then they have to think about how to drop dead weight and restructure the managerial pyramid, transfer control to those who can handle it, and shift from threat to motivation so as not to lose momentum.

I've stated that a dispute only has meaning when the participants are in agreement as to the understanding of the subject up for debate. Let's begin by clarifying the question: Is a System necessary to improve the overall result or for us to divvy up that result correctly? We still need to achieve a good result to have something to share later, following our understanding of the principles of justice. Otherwise, it won't work.

It can be assumed that our overall result will grow on its own if we simply do everything in matters of state structure as is customary "among civilized people", which is to say, as they do in more economically successful countries. No one, however, remembers the flaws in the practical organization of our economic interaction that we spoke about. If the expenses and losses born of these flaws aren't going anywhere, then what's going to suddenly improve our economic result? Moreover, for the most part, these flaws can be identified even without entering into politics and waiting for the next election campaign.

Judging by the content of the controversy and election programs in Russia, we're more concerned about how we share the results. Especially when it comes to the contents of the Big Body's pocket, which we generally receive from the sale of raw materials for export. It looks like a paradox when an inveterate liberal economist promises to achieve economic growth by making withdrawals from the state budget or from abstract corrupt officials, oligarchs, developers, and retailers—in short, from everyone who probably receives "extra"—and to divide these funds in some "correct" way. All that's needed to accomplish this is installing the "right person" at the head of the state machine. That means that their audience, or potential electorate, are freedom-loving people who will be satisfied with the state if they can count on the handouts promised by their candidate. No, sorry, not a handout, but a certain share. There's just no method of calculating this share that has anything to do with the economy. The calculation is rather based on the ghostly possibility of bargaining to get what you want.

Nothing arouses public interest like money in someone else's hands, so the most widely discussed problem is corruption. This sin is as ancient as other manifestations of human weakness, and nobody has yet been able to defeat it once and for all. The fight against this evil becomes a good means for self-expression, for vivid, highfalutin rhetoric, and a convenient instrument of blackmail and coercion for the System itself.

It's worth taking a detour from the corrupted—this character who is to blame for everything—and to look at the "twilight zone" created through common efforts in which even the simplest problem cannot be resolved simply. Our baseline conditions are rules initially loaded with contradictions, constantly changing, and often unfeasible in practice. The basic algorithms are constructed in such a way that, at any moment, a System representative can find a subject for discussion, a reason for compromise, and the inevitable bargaining with anyone trying to get a move on. This is simply an ideal environment for corruption.

From the economic perspective, if a bribe brings the result one step closer to realization, that's better than losses from slowdowns or stoppages of economic processes caused by the System falling into a safe and familiar state of stupor. Then money is already irrevocably flushing down the drain. If the result is achieved nonetheless, then the bribe is money that can then be found and even partially paid back.

So far, it looks like we're determined to root out and expose offenders until we're blue in the face. I remember the creation of state "regulators of regulators," who referred to themselves as the vanguard in the fight against evil, was announced. But after a few steps in, it turns out they weren't much different than those they were hunting. If you replace the guards in uniform with vigilant volunteers, I'm not sure the chances of success increase. Instead, pile-ons by activists will become an integral part of the problem, and a flurry of denunciations and demonstrative flogging of apostates will fail to result in significant progress. At the end of the day, we'll reach another managerial impasse with no safe way out.

The actions of whistleblowers and the state machine sometimes synchronize in strange ways. For example, when a contractor has to be driven to take on a problematic project and then made to pay for the stupidity and mistakes of others, an anti-corruption investigation will appear out of nowhere—and then disappear just as suddenly when the contractor takes a plea deal.

So long as we're determined to exchange all bad people, such as bribers, for fair and good ones, then the matter clearly will not be limited to replacing the most important and corrupt ones. The problem is where to find one more, two, a hundred thousand or a million "quality" candidates at once. The most obvious solution is suggested by Asian tradition or the *Game of Thrones* series: In order to make bureaucrats unsullied and to immunize them against temptation, one must first confiscate their testicles. Yet another question remains – how does it work with female candidates?

If we're looking for a surefire way to improve human nature, then, personally, I'll pass. After all, if the choice is between an idealist with little understanding of what can be done and how to do it, or a pragmatic cynic who can evaluate the results of action or inaction, who should be entrusted with decision-making power? I'm for the competent cynic. Otherwise, we'll get the usual feeling of dissonance—the words will seem correct, the rituals just the same, everything as it is "among civilized people," but, in practice, something so familiar hurts...

A perfect candidate with a heart of gold can be installed at the top of the pyramid and can say all the right words. In order for the images, they draw to become reality, besides this leader and their apostles from campaign headquarters, many thousands of people, far from ideal, must be involved directly in the process of state governance. It is only possible when all good intentions are transformed into clear management algorithms.

To fix a mistake, you must first learn how to find it. A large part of the problem can be solved in its correct formulation by eradicating all errors from the rules governing the System's operations, starting with the most obvious, to which we devoted several of the previous chapters. Fighters for radical change, however, ignore these "trivial and boring" details with the same obstinacy as their opponents. Copying schemas, procedures, rituals, and rhetoric is offered up as the key to success and a solution to problems. Then the critics have shown themselves to understand the subject no better and make the same fundamental mistakes as those they're criticizing. The focus then shifts to simple, ready-made answers, reflecting an abstract, correct idea with the same old weak, practical study and vague chances of success.

There's a common metaphor involving a cargo cult in which an airbase was built on Melanesian islands somewhere in the Pacific during World War II. Airplanes landed there, and a portion of their cargo was given to the locals for their help and the inconvenience. After the airbase was shut down, the locals continued to look after it, building idols like life-size replicas of airplanes out of straw, mimicking the day-to-day activities and dress styles of U.S. soldiers, and waiting for the delivery of delicious food like before. Critics of the System like to use this metaphor without thinking about how they're simply calling the audience to a different straw "airplane."

Each time, it becomes harder and harder to make a big wave in a small puddle. We get excited right around the time of the next campaign, hoping to resolve everything once and for all, making the right choice. Between these events, passions slowly smolder and flare up, reacting to the next awkward turn of the System as to an inflamed and leaking abscess. Opponents of the System don't have a convincing diagnosis of their own or an understanding of what to do, no meaningful rallying cry. Fighters of the System go voluntarily to uncertain ground, where they're not liable to have a confident argument: to the realm of debates on the best world order and the personal qualities of individuals. They periodically take center stage only to lose spectacularly once again.

The tyrant and incarnation of evil can only nod thoughtfully from a safe distance while their opponents do all the work for them. The situation is well-known to anyone familiar with contact sports—it's extremely clear who has the initiative. All that dictator needs is to maintain the points lead, flawlessly manipulating and forcing the enemy to bend to the whims of their own emotions.

It's easy to lose the main thread when carried away by abstract definitions, discussing all issues in "general terms," immediately on a large scale. We're talking about human units who, within the bounds of a single country, are united by common goals, territory, and so on. We never cease to be human first and foremost. This is who we are. The state and society, bureaucrats and businesspeople, managers and the managed, buyers and sellers—these are all just functions we perform, or the roles offered to us by the System. As soon as we stop seeing the people behind these generalizing designations and classifications, the conversation gradually devolves into an empty exercise in rhetoric.

If we want to construct actually inclusive institutions, then it's only possible when everybody who is involved understands his responsibility. We just copy these institutes, being excited by the success of others—we would rather lose because such a scheme is more difficult in practice for all participants. We slip back to archaic centralized forms under the name of formal democracy without any conspiracies, it happens itself when we choose the easiest way too often. In order to solve complex problems, we create our own System based on a certain general idea that we have agreed is correct. But that's just an assumption that must be verified in practice. It's not enough to choose an attractive idea, to latch onto a fortuitous thought. For everything to work, we need to think further. The idea should be understood and thought through by everyone individually—not "believed in," but *thought about*. If that's not done, the idea will fizzle out.

No, it'll remain the most correct, justifying the endless "That's how it should be!" Our System, constructed around the "most correct idea," will once again become a cumbersome, useless pyramid. At the very base alone, there might remain a small chamber at the very base containing the right ideas and plans that were initially supposed to unite everyone, inspire hope, and direct them toward a goal. Now it is nothing but a symbol of faith and a perfect instrument in the struggle for power.

Do we need to hold our heads so high all the time to find answers up there, or, at least, some clues? Would it perhaps be worth looking ahead or to the side to see if there's something just as interesting there?

What if the answers we're looking for aren't somewhere out there in the realm of big numbers and scientific terminology, but much closer, at arm's length? What if we shouldn't direct our questions somewhere up above, into the void, but to somebody who's just passing by right now? Big figures and the overall result is nothing but the sum of interaction between elementary particles of the System—between human beings. Each of them tries to construct their relationship with all others like. Let's look at this task and, first of all, clear up a working space of distractions, of all parts that we are not able to define clearly and objectively.

~ CHAPTER TWELVE ~
ALL KIDDING ASIDE

For a person living among other people, limits and obligations are unavoidable. When this person does not feel constrained as far as they can accept these obligations as understandable and adequate, they can dispute and clarify the terms of their contract with the System, but they can't reject the necessity of the deal itself, under which terms they must pay with the hours of their life. To keep the System from overloading them, a conversation is needed between them both that puts "all kidding aside," avoiding impossible promises from either end. Freedom has a downside—the recognition that nobody owes anyone else anything just like that. The liberal idea in this form will never lose its edge. It's not an empty slogan, but an approach to building a working schema that minimizes the size and weight of the control hierarchy subject to the fulfillment of the general tasks as they've been set forth.

Russian mass media stubbornly broadcast the same image with slight variations. Serious people in suits are doing the almost impossible for us: Uplifting the economy, harvests, the birthrate and, in general, helping us to "get off the ground." The task isn't easy, but the wording is impeccable and the creases between their brows have the same tense quality as those on the granite those on the granite Atlases that the artist Terebenev installed to hold up the Hermitage Palace. These people in suits speak and write to each other while virtuously avoiding real action. The most streamlined formulations have little to do with practice. Still, that's only half the trouble. It's worse when these characters start to believe that everything's working and that it'll turn out well solely because they spew the right words so convincingly. For example, as in the case of the assumption of the head of government that someday soon we'll reach such a high level of digitization and robotization that we'll be able to tack on an extra day off for our fellow citizens. It's good that we can rest while imaginary robots do imaginary work for us. But nobody specified that our well-being would also remain imaginary.

Reality leaves a feeling of the proverbial cognitive dissonance because nothing changes. All these phrases, pronounced and printed in hundreds of documents, weighty, all smooth edges, fall and roll with a booming noise to dissolve in the sediment of other accumulated useless, correct words.

It's worth watching and listening to those nearer to you. They don't need to be raised from the ground because they're not kneeling on it—not because they're proud, but because they've got work to do. They do the work not because they were directed to, but have been told endlessly how important and correct it is. More than once, they have started from nothing and gathered up their lives from fragments, not wasting time and energy searching for excuses but finding out what else could be done and trying not to let anyone down. They haven't lost themselves, though they've been lost more than once by the System during its repeated crises.

Most astonishing is that, despite everything, these people have retained the ability to feel joy and bring happiness to those around them. If you look and listen closely, everyone has a story—and what a story it is!

These people have been able to do the most fundamental thing: They didn't become "lost," they didn't once ask the sacred question of "Do I need it?" but rather formed the scaffolding that kept the entire economy from crumbling and saved the System itself. They are the statistical majority, but if there were a percent or two fewer of such people, the whole System would fail and the characters on TV would have nothing to talk about, just convinced of their powerlessness. They are the country's most important economic reserve: People who go to work every day and contribute something useful. These people who don't let anyone down fulfill the necessary conditions for weathering any crisis—they bear the whole load on their shoulders. These people deplore both adherents of the centralized System and its overthrowers equally, as both types rob them of a well-deserved victory.

On a TV show, the most active chatterbox tossed out the idea that throughout the election campaign, citizens were voting for the ability to consume. The rest of the guests discussed this pronouncement with him for another good half hour. First of all, everyone acquires their ability to consume at the same place where they exchange hours of their life for money, multiplied by their energy and abilities, trying to do what someone else needs. All the other people around them are doing the same. It seems we almost forget about this fact in order to engage in abstract reasoning about who owes whom and how much, which is appropriate for such TV shows.

The System itself has little interest in what happens to the majority as long as the difficult and boring process of creating a small fraction of the overall result takes place in these jobs, in the "rest" of the economy. The final figures or significant "high-tech" vectors, into which it will transfer funds from the Big Body, are more important to it. It is, however, safe to expect that the System will arrive for its share as soon as cash starts to appear.

If we want to debug our System and correct its internal algorithms, then it's better to lay off politics. We ought to start with what we do every working day, not once every four years. Then the ideas presented as the most correct in the course of election campaigns will acquire some meaning and chances for implementation. I'm not certain it's necessary just to overthrow or replace anyone in order to take the first step in the right direction.

We're building a System that can raise our overall result and will not resort to grubby cheating when this result is divided up. The System helps everyone to build relationships with everyone else, including with those to whom nothing connects us directly. We might be separated by a multitude of intermediate links and transactions, but everyone should receive what's theirs. The relationship each of us has with all the rest is the source material, the "elementary particle," for building the System.

I propose starting by resolving the most important question: Who owes whom and how much at the level of any given individual? If the answer is described using a comprehensible system of equations that can be solved, then the System's source material takes on volume, shape, and solidity. Any System we draw for ourselves in general terms while the search for an answer to this question devolves into endless polemicizing will result in disappointment. We can model our System on those of other countries that outpace us economically or invent something of our own, but if we haven't solved this problem, we'll still just be building "sandcastles."

I'll share a terrible secret with you. I myself am a subject with limited rationality. Severely limited. I demonstrate that every time I bargain with my own body: I want to watch a show and have some beer and chips, but it needs an hour of torment on the cardio machine. The prospect of bringing closer the day when my capricious body will start to fail and severely limit my choice of available options. Why, it'll be the day when I'm no longer able to be surprised or happy, when I lose the ability to search and move forward. That'll be the day when I really begin to die.

I can negotiate with myself, even find a common language with loved ones, but how can I force myself to do the right thing rather than the convenient one when it comes to total strangers? Especially if the rules by which I'm supposed to orient myself are taken as conventions, dictated by some other person who claims, "That's how it should be," and not based on objective knowledge or common sense. It helps to understand that every time I choose to be disingenuous in fulfilling my obligations to others, I bring closer that moment when I'll have to flee from my responsibility for broken promises and mistakes rather than work to create more opportunities.

That's if the System is functioning. It can't make us honest. It's enough if the System increases the chances of someone deciding against pulling a fast one on others and themselves.

When the System doesn't function, you have to lie harder or more shrewdly each time in order to retain your position while negative selection is in effect. Or try to occupy a post that allows you to dump your responsibilities on others and continue to exploit the flaws in System algorithms. The most difficult and practically impossible task remains acting according to what the knowledge you've gained in the course of professional training and common sense suggests.

One time during a trip to Germany, I asked an Albanian

who'd been working there decently for a long time how he liked it. It turned out he didn't like it at all. He had to live in Macedonia, where he had a chic house and a Mercedes but worked in Germany. Because over there it was clear what he needed to do and how much he'd get paid if he played by the rules. Was it really just like that, according to the rules? Judging by his sly smirk, not quite, but my interlocutor also had a good understanding of who could catch him in a lie, how, and just how much he'd have to pay were it to happen.

Another friend of mine added an important detail to this schema. When the Soviet Union fell apart, the armed forces fell apart with it. Like thousands of other officers, he couldn't find a place for himself in the wreckage of the once-impressive army and eventually ended up in Germany, living hand to mouth. As a semi-legal migrant, he could find work at small construction sites for private contractors, where he learned how to lay tiles. Gradually, he got back on his feet and decided to start as an independent contractor. But this turned out not to be so simple. In order to take contracts so as not to be dependent on shady offers, he needed to get an education and a place in the local professional guild. After a few years, having spent tens of thousands of German marks, he received, along with his title, a knowledge of the rules governing how titles are customarily laid in this land (mark) in exchange for money. Moreover, the guild is indicated as an arbitrator in contracts there. In the event of a dispute, a representative of the guild (essentially, the master teacher), comes and checks how well the lessons have been learned, and the court accepts the determination of the guild. If the lessons have been learned poorly, you can forget about the money. Clearly, this practice doesn't make life any easier for novices.

This inconvenient set-up had to eventually be examined from another angle in 2012, when the German market opened up to the labor force from the EU8 countries, new members of the European Union from the former socialist camp.

The expectations of the "locals" (including my friend) were exceedingly pessimistic. The first thing the guests did was to lower prices aggressively and take a significant portion of the work. They weren't obliged to anyone for anything, nobody demanded they deal with the guild, that amusing local anachronism. An interesting thing happened when the "guest workers" began trying to peddle the results of their work. The clients had not forgotten the rules by which the result must be evaluated and began to use any deviation as an excuse simply not to pay. When the guests were faced with the necessity of clarifying local requirements and fulfilling them in full, the work no longer seemed so simple to them. As a result, their offers became more expensive, and the market gradually recovered. Certainly not to the previous level—prices have fallen, but to a tolerable state, and those locals who remained professional have retained their positions and avoided the fate of "lost people."

A person needs an understanding of what they must know and be able to do so that an hour of their life is not worth the minimum ten coins for a set of arms and legs and the ability to move them according to a simple set of instructions, but fifteen, twenty, and so on. For them, these are the initial conditions of the problem: How to find and take their place in the general matrix while extracting maximum benefit for themselves. This rigid, often inconvenient construction helps them to find support and prevents them from falling through the cracks. The more incomprehensible conventions and unfulfillable promises there are in this schema, the faster it becomes blurred, and we get, again, that same "Lost Boy" instead of an engineer, welder, technologist, or plumber. As the practices of recent years demonstrate, in our cities, even the competent janitor can fade away.

Ultimately corporations, associations, and even the state are nothing more than organizational forms that allow some people to make decisions for others and to act on their behalf. Everything the economy operates on, at the end of the day, is what one person does and another one pays for. These terms add up to the overall result (for clarity, we can recall the GDP). If we're not able to cover all our obligations to others by means of work, and are still indebted to someone, then there's something wrong with our equation. Or it's not about money. Everyone adds their contribution to this sum and can't withdraw more than what they put in. On the contrary, a little has to be left over for insurance. As you get older, you understand that you're quite lucky if you're just healthy and not constantly looking for work. So be ready to share with those less fortunate, help them not to give up, and then you can expect some reciprocal courtesy.

We're not talking about old people, children, or the sick—we're talking about healthy, mature adults. The question is, from whom can they expect or demand bonuses, and is it worth trusting those who promise this bonus during political campaigns?

Dear human beings... Wake up. Look around. There are thousands more like you listening to the same fairytales. Those who promised them justice and equity can't find enough to share with everyone. For more than 200 years, this word has been written on flags, but, from a practical point of view, economic justice remains a subjective concept with a pronounced emotional connotation. It has no direct relation to any discussion about the economy, and any attempt to build a System guided by the principle of justice is an attempt to solve the problem in a manner that no one will ever be able to.

When we expect justice from the System, we're trying to endow it with a poorly defined function. An incomprehensible variable appears in the equation: national wealth or inheritance, something that seems to exist and can be shared. If we're told about some common thing, divorced from the source, from the task for which it was gathered, that means someone who can't be trusted wants to have control of the money. Usually, we're talking about the Big Bag, and the applicant for the System's most important position has promised to find a solution there. At first, they promise to fill the Big Bag with money that they'll get from some third party. They'll cite extensive criteria: Funds should be gathered from corporations, oligarchs, corrupt officials—from anyone at all, except from you, a citizen with a developed sense of justice. And you listen and imagine how good it'll be for you. Just keep both hands in your pockets. There are people just like you crowding around, and for them, your money is also "someone else's."

Why can we expect something inexplicable from the state, like from a magic pot in which there's enough porridge for everyone? Sure, theoretically, our ancestors provided us with control over the territory, subjugating or driving someone else's ancestors into the desert, forests, or tundra. Thanks very much for that. But even the resources mined in this territory only become money when someone pays for them and digs into their own pockets to do so. As a result, everything is paid for by someone who also had to do something for someone else, it doesn't matter who—a compatriot or a foreigner. In the end, everything once again comes down to that primary transaction in which a person exchanges a part of their life for money. Ultimately, the System in which this process is better organized wins the economic competition. On the other hand, in a well-organized System everyone can more accurately determine their portion of the overall result, and the chances of getting that portion increase.

If we return to attempts to correct the System during election campaigns, then following this logic, the System must take something from somewhere so that the winning candidate can pay for the support of those who voted for them with this "something." Candidates will manipulate these promises endlessly such that they're never entirely fulfilled. The promised share of some common something will attract anyone weaker. The formulas for success, on closer inspection, look more like a chimp's imitation or a journey down a mystical path that doesn't conform to the laws we learned in school. Where's the schema that provides support and guidelines for decision-making for anyone?

Better approaches seem to be known in countries where there are fewer subsoil resources, territory, and commonwealth, but where nonetheless the result per person is significantly higher. Not everything is easy there, either. Conditions change with increasing speed, and almost everyone periodically has to look for a new place and new content to use his time and energy. Doing so is easier if there are clues and support, such as an answer to the question "What do I have to do?" like using training wheels on a bike for the first time to go further. It's better if painful changes occur in the course of a game that operates by clear rules. It's easier to take on the burden and responsibility if the System doesn't confuse a palm tree for a cow, if it doesn't lie to itself and force others to as well. If this System doesn't work, then what are we talking about with these thousands of people in uniforms and suits explaining to us how to do everything right?

For one complex question about our social structure or politics, there are a thousand simpler issues at the level of economic or administrative interaction that each of us must resolve daily and hourly. Most of these issues involve the relationship between two people—buyer and seller. And so long as these two have neither the desire nor the ability to get by without the participation of a third party, who is dominant, the huge hierarchical pyramid will grow at a steady pace.

Let me reiterate: The overall result of the System's construction depends on the material from which it is built. These are the same people who, when making choices, do so only in response to pressure from above, leaving the initiative to someone powerful without whom they cannot manage. The building material remains free-flowing and amorphous, unsuitable for building horizontal bonds. Each element carries the load placed on it from above, and this is as if pressed from all sides. We try our best to reproduce other models, copying procedures, rituals, technology, and methods; we repeat, like incantations, formulas for success, but again we build our pyramid. Then we just recount that slightly remastered old story about the "Leviathan-state" that English philosopher Thomas Hobbes told some 300 years ago.

A meaningful conversation begins with a discussion of a functional schema that allows for the distribution of functions, workload, and responsibility among everyone. It remains to make the basis of this contract rigid, but clear, or no motivation will work. It's not a market economy, not capitalism or socialism, but just the economy in its most essential sense: the interaction of people engaged in their own or common exchange of resources. Any other design, even one based on the brightest of ideas, will not be viable.

So, as far as we have clarified the issue of construction material, we can revise the design of the System itself.

Dmitry Eremenko

~ CHAPTER THIRTEEN ~
IN SEARCH OF SUPPORT

For us to rely on the System, we must first restore its governability. Even primates can build simple hierarchies. We differ from them in that we can set ourselves more complex common tasks for the long term and build schemas of interaction that allow these tasks to be resolved while we remain aware of what we're doing. As a result, those at the very top ought to be making sure that everything is working out, not just giving instructions and endowing them with the highest priority. If the formulation of the task is too vague, if feedback is silenced or replaced by an imitation signal, then obedience takes up more attention and resources and gradually replaces management. Thus, bosses both big and small will indicate the size of their ego. Instead of performing useful functions, all efforts will be spent on fighting for positions in the power hierarchy. Instead of solving large and complex problems, accompanied by incredibly clever words and complex rituals, in reality, only the most ancient and primitive of tasks will be solved. Actually, a group of baboons could handle that in the same way.

If the solution to all practical problems is left to the whim of the state, and each time we try finding answers at the very top of the power vertical, then it'll only be possible to cause a few convulsions that spread throughout the Big Body. Don't forget that we're asking those very same people who've successfully distorted and bent the algorithms to suit them. By relying on the solution to the problem from above, we risk each time getting another formalized description of how the solution looks from the very top instead of a logical algorithm. This description will be replete with words like *ought, must,* and *should,* and will depict in detail how the establishment of an imaginary order in an imaginary country looks from a bird's eye view. The most tenacious people risk getting a new set of rules that'll be understood best by the prosecutor's office and the investigative committee. At any level, the decision can be substituted for a trick that produces a result ranging anywhere from nothing to the rather negative, then issuing all that as another directive, law, order, or standard. And if we just need a recommendation or some advice, what's a reason to invite some powerful person?

This was one of the lessons I learned in the Soviet army. Stars on epaulets conferred the ability to order and punish, but did not guarantee that all orders would be carried out. The strengthening of discipline often looked like a boring ritual: The alpha male, by position and rank, shouted orders of what he wanted and what he would do to his subordinates if his orders were unfulfilled. Moreover, he described, quite vividly, his pathologies and simplistic sexual fantasies in which his subordinates and all their immediate relatives would be participating. This part was occasionally not boring and sometimes even terrifying—when the commander, for example, throws a person standing nearby in line onto the floor, laying into his body with a series of blows, then turns to you, as a junior colleague, and explains, "Don't hit them in the mouth, it'll leave marks. And not in the jaw either, it might break...." Except everyone knows that nothing will change, and everything will repeat itself day after day—a stupefying, exhausting routine, generously seasoned with stress and humiliation. For some, it'll end in a year or two, but for others, it'll drag on for almost a lifetime.

When you give an order, you start a story that you must finish yourself. Everyone needs to understand this: You yourself, and those who are supposed to obey you. If that's not the case, better shut up and think about it. Exercising authority, giving strict orders, and establishing rigid control isn't management yet. It won't do to confuse management and obedience. Management aims to achieve a common goal, and it begins when each participant understands how they will handle their part of the common task, and what they need to accomplish it beyond diligence, faith, and devotion.

It's better to find the malfunction in the System and to fix the error itself than to correct its effects. So, let's once again start with simple and understandable tasks, as they have everything the employees need to provide the System with an adequate, readable feedback signal. It is just a basis of any control process, and the very existence of such a signal is a necessary condition for moving forward in the right direction. It remains to combine the concrete task in its correct formulation with the rules written for those who will have to solve this problem without needlessly appealing to the power vertical. Everything required for this can be found in textbooks, with which only those who've read them and understood nothing or haven't bothered to read them at all can argue.

While I was searching for a common language with our permit system, the German Code of Rules (*Regelwerk*) fell into my lap to help me perform the calculations I needed. These rules were drafted by a national association that includes all the relevant parties: customers, builders, designers, and materials manufacturers. This association has tens of thousands of members, and a humble office handles ongoing organizational work. How do they do it? They determine the practical task and gather together a group of twenty-four leading experts to draft a project document. After these twenty-four smart people agree (a process that might take several years), the document is offered up for discussion to association members at large. The rules for this discussion are the same as before—only objective comments and only on the nature of the proposed practical task. When all comments are resolved, the final version is approved and published. The document is reviewed if there are good reasons to do so, or else every three years—just in case.

It's very similar in form to our technical committees that I mentioned in the first chapter. Except here, during the discussion of a technical problem, for some reason, they debate it on its merits without running a risk to their professional reputation. The group might include competitors or representatives from companies between whom there are ongoing court proceedings. If they're unable to leave their disputes at the door, they're politely asked to leave and not invited back. This successful calculation model or method created by the professional association is equally suitable for solving similar problems anywhere, in the hands of any specialist who understands what kind of tool it is. It turns out that almost the whole world has copied their homework off the Anglo-Saxons, Germans, and French and by no means has an inferiority complex. Those who need to translate these documents into their own language and make use of them, like the Chinese, for example. Might we also do so? Well, sure. All limitations are within the bounds of copyright. I can translate and use content, but print and sales of copies is a prerogative of the German association.

Now for the most treacherous question. We must clarify the status of the document. Who approved it, and who obliged us to respect and comply with these rules? It has to be a certain representative of the powerful System, according to my previous experience. And here's where I ran into complete failure. I was unable to find any papers with a solid seal and signature. So, who declared this rules document official, who monitors the observance of these rules and metes out punishment for their infringement? Practically no one.

The corpus of rules was not approved by any specially authorized person, none of those to whom prosecutors and inspectors must report; not even the deputy minister signed it. So, who will fulfill these obligations, then? Ah, well, it's Germany, everyone there has a certain mentality and is obsessed with order, according to a popular cliché.

Once again, I guessed wrong. Rules are about how work should be done such that everyone will be satisfied with the result. If we understand the question, we know how to answer it, and then what more can a person with a position in the state hierarchy tell us? It's customary to refer to the rules in contracts or project documents so that it's clear what's been taken as the basis for solving the problem. A maverick who considers themselves above these rules will find it difficult to get orders and even more difficult to find payment for their work. The same rules are invoked when it comes to dealings with the state or going to court.

If specialists can't set for themselves a bottom line beyond which a product is no longer a product, work is no longer work for which money or even a "thank you" can be expected, then what kind of specialists are they? Draw this boundary in such a manner that nobody can move it or make it pliable and permeable, as we described in the chapter about clear rules. Then there will be no possibility of compromising with yourself and haggling with the regulator to move bids "under the table," where the winner will be the one who doesn't get caught or the smoothest talker. There will certainly be those people who want to argue with expert opinion: either the powerful state representatives themselves, whose food supply has just been downsized, or, on the other side of the coin, those players who are prevented from doing shady dealings by rules that are too comprehensible.

We need common tasks wherein authorities are only called in to help find a solution as necessary. That's a normal division in any control system. Subordinates can and should have their own internal structure and internal algorithms that allow them to provide upper levels with a normal, readable signal rather than just reacting with a desperate squeak as they're crushed. It's not enough to say that we don't like something. We have to propose our own solution and show that, in this case, we can steer everything to port in the end ourselves. This, if you like, is an indicator of maturity, that ability to say: "Dad, I'll do it myself..." We have to say it, and we have to manage on our own.

We find support in an area where it's better for the power vertical not to adjust the rules for itself or to dictate things. All the state needs to support this division is a genuine interest in improving the overall result and not just constructing useless verticals. This area is forming its own, independent part of the System. It is constantly at work, not activated from time to time to participate in political campaigns or to express protest—there are more than enough practical tasks to fill the agenda. Along the edge of this area, a dividing line appears, fulfilling practically the same function as the Rubicon did in ancient Rome. On one side of it, the imperium (an ancient Roman set of powers with which Caesar did not wish to part) does not work.

Here we're talking on equal footing with the state about issues that we discussed above and the rules that will enable us to resolve them.

There's now an opportunity for meaningful dialogue with the power vertical, one that provides the chance for the full powers of the authorities to be used for their intended purpose.

If you, a respected representative of the powerful part of our System, are trying to guard something against encroachment, please be so kind as to clearly define what you'll consider a crime and what comprehensible, calculable harm such an act might cause. If you can't, don't rush to canonize another confusing decree by which measure any one of us could wind up beyond the "red line." Your law will simply not be enforced and the harm that could result from this might be extensive.

There are a number of tasks we've already dealt with on our side of the Rubicon, and it's unlikely that the state can add anything of substance to our resolution. Our rules are based on an understanding of the task, on common sense, and on laws that it's useless to argue with. Even if the state sees discrepancies, there's no need to rush to put things in order and impose their version of how everything should be arranged. Especially if dozens of approved documents could be expressed in several different formulas and none of these formulas can be replaced in any way. A state representative can make some comments on the form, but if they don't want to look like an idiot, then they should leave the contents alone.

The state doesn't get anywhere on wishes and advice; "heavy argumentation" interferes. Our interactions are set up in such a way that signals from above (or, from the other side of the Rubicon) do not come in the form of recommendations but rather as directives: If you do this, nothing will happen to you, but if you don't, it'll hurt. For directives to be meaningful, they must be comprehensible and enforceable. They shouldn't look like ambiguous and contradictory canonical texts we have no hope of understanding without help from on high. Furthermore, these laws and standards shouldn't be constantly changing and being added to. Yesterday, we were given your permission, but today it's worthless, just like your word. Yesterday, what we were doing was correct, but now suddenly the concept has changed, and we find ourselves in violation. Explain or define "who foots the bill." Is the new limit line so important, or is the problem so acute as to justify all of us losing money from a sudden change in the rules of the game?

If you see something going wrong, the first step is to identify the threat, evaluate it, and compare the potential damage with the total expense of restoring order. Otherwise, you're just wasting money. Those of us who don't follow the new bend in the road will reset ourselves and nullify all our obligations. Those who survive will try to pass these expenses on to others. Even a demolished little kiosk results in losses for buyers as well as owners. Customers will now have to spend an extra five rubles or five minutes to find and purchase what they need. It is, in fact, economic losses anyway. Against the backdrop of such senseless waste, your calls and plans to improve the overall economic result look like a mockery.

The state representative intervenes in the management of economic processes to cut costs and catch violators, referring back to their own logic. They force the product to be substituted with something similar that's been approved and is cheaper, or they stop and prohibit another product, not having found the right word in their canonical texts. Then they report on the successes they've achieved: millions in damages prevented and money saved. A plan or a project differs from good intentions if it is drawn up in such a way that it can be carried out to completion and achieve an economic effect. The main thing is to calculate the total result in conjunction with those who will be fulfilling these plans. Then delays and downtime will be added while the System "ponders." Let's also add expenses for projects that were delayed or even canceled because a new governor took office or the System once again "changed its mind" like the extra floors of buildings in Sankt-Petersburg that were suddenly cut off by "skyline," set at a height of forty meters. Add on the money that was spent on correcting errors in the plans deformed to your dictation. Take the total amount and the time that has elapsed since the initial incursion of the expenses, multiply it by at least the refinancing rate of the Central Bank, and then we'll find out just how much we've all lost thanks to the tireless work of establishing order.

Nothing is free for us, and nothing is free for you, my powerful colleague. Somehow, your itch and urge to establish order have to be brought to heel. Picture this: Even if you don't correct and regulate at least one thing every day, not everything is bound to collapse. Perhaps the official and volunteer guardians of the order will get upset. The first will spend less time at the trough and the second won't have much excuse to bawl. While the majority will breathe easier.

Do you understand the meaning of the processes you're trying to manage or are you just doing your due diligence, formulating the task in such a way that, just in case, you can always cover your ass with one document or another?

As soon as we achieve any kind of economic result, then the state is the first to take its share. The address and purpose of this money is not a concept in broad terms that has its own goals and an enlightened consciousness, but quite specific people who resolve certain problems. If we turn not to these people but to some abstract powerful System for confidence and security in the future, then both our confidence and our security will be just as abstract. The first warning sign is when, time after time, they say that they'll do their best and try their utmost. If they promise everything at once, then, more often than not, nothing happens. Or should we play the same trick on the state that we played on ourselves—trying to give it and its responsibilities weight and form?

Why should we believe in a complex schema with a wealth of derivatives if we see neither the desire nor the ability to begin with something simple and comprehensible? The state has always been paid for and is still being paid for, in the first order, safety. Once upon a time, the protection it provided was purely physical, but now we've expanded this concept, adding, in particular, a certain guaranteed level of education as well as medical and social security. The result that can be obtained depends on the availability of limited resources and our capacity to use them. We give money to the state to fulfill this task. The level of security we can afford depends on the overall result and on how overburdened the entire schema is by mismanagement, parasites, and "lost people."

And, please, spare the dramatic effects and the hopes that we'll be made confident and satisfied. Yes, we're still being helped to raise the birthrate. Maybe we'll multiply more cheerfully when we finally feel this security, and not because this endeavor is elevated to the rank of a national project, and everyone gets a little money for it. One thing will have to be clarified—is it possible to still have fun while doing it, if everything is so serious? I don't know about you, but as soon as I remember national ideas and strategic tasks, my fertility plummets.

If we have tasks in common with the state, then so does the System that helps to solve them. We are part of the System ourselves, after all. On our side of the Rubicon, we take on simpler functions and occupy the System's lower floors. We make sure our part of the structure carries the necessary loads, but here we also build at our discretion cantilevers, arches, and spans for freedom of movement and redistribution of the total weight. We build it up and change it as we see fit, following external signals.

We want the part of the System on the other side of the Rubicon to be able to formulate clearly its tasks and really solve them. That way, it'll be easier to trust that it can handle the more complex problems that actually are better seen from the top and to accept subordination as a reasonable necessity.

That's how we stop viewing the state as a kind of given or as a higher power—we must ask and wait for it to grant our hopes. Now, our Rubicon can be crossed in any direction by anyone who has proven their ability to resolve the practical issues of management without, at the same time, choosing between the "dark" or the "light" side. Those on the upper floors are no longer a group of chosen ones dealing in secret knowledge who lead, personify, and embody. Now that abstract "something" that directs our lives becomes what it really is—a group of people with their own functions and powers who are also subordinated to the achievement of a common goal.

There is one necessary condition. This schema is more complex, so everyone will have to think and engage; otherwise it won't work. As soon as we forget about this, that "subject with limited rationality" in each of us, resembling a chimp in its habits, wakes up. It serves as a constant reminder that without conscious effort regarding oneself, copying complex schemas from other communities is pointless. There are no ready-made answers, no ideal System that will work correctly even when it's not being used by an ideal person.

ASKING THE RIGHT QUESTIONS

~ CHAPTER FOURTEEN ~
READY-MADE ANSWERS
(or, "Among Civilized People")

There is no sense in bothering my readers with stories about the transformation of the Soviet Union to modern Russia. But they can easily recognize how the same or comparable processes go on abroad, following the same logic and limited rationality of non-ideal people. One such example is Latin America, where they rush from one extreme version of the right general concept to the other and cannot solve the social problems. The difference is how far we can go ahead following an abstract scheme, which we suggest is the last version of the truth, and ignoring our practical mistakes and weaknesses.

I like products of modern streaming services, especially based on real cases such as *The Dropout* and *Dopesick*. The first one shows Elizabeth Holmes as the ideal Mimic who used flawless performance instead of real research and development. The second is the case of OxyContin, that opioid-based painkiller that was promoted in the U.S. as practically harmless. Here was the same tricky manipulation with formalized regulation procedures and human belief in official approvals, as discussed above. I think, if anybody suggests that their society is absolutely immune to such effects just because they possess passports of different colors, then they are cheating themselves.

I also prefer discussing more abstract issues —like how things work with "other people" and why, exactly, they are "other." You can toss out one after another deep, empty maxim about some abstract, typical Japanese or Moldovan person to pass as an intellectual. To better understand the reasons behind the economic successes of others and the failures of our own, we ought to just pull back the curtain of the usual stereotypes and see how similar we are. Let's still work off the supposition that all people are fundamentally the same. Long gone are the times when in certain parts of the world people didn't have the wheel and somewhere else, they didn't know about black powder weaponry. These days, practically the entire world is attempting to resolve the same types of issues using the same universally available tools. For some people, things turn out better, for some worse, but we're hardly going to find answers by blindly copying off others' homework—including all the errors.

In 2003, a colleague and I were flying through Damascus to Aleppo on a business trip. For the first time, in lieu of the familiar ticket printed on a tear-off sheet of carbon paper (there were such things then), we were given a printout on a standard piece of paper. The agency assured us that this would be more than enough to get us on the flight and added that we had nothing to fear. Eventually, late at night in the Damascus airport, we threw ourselves at every person in uniform with this printout and the request that they show us who, specifically, could assist. All of them directed us to an empty table in the corner of the terminal with a computer in a slipcover on it, nodded, and then made calming gestures with their hands. Time passed, but we crowded around the empty table. So far, we had not decided it was pointless to keep waiting and break through security to the gate.

In this part of the airport, we barely managed to get our boarding passes and, in a disheveled state, dashed to the gate. Now all we had to do was get through the gauntlet of three intimidating officers performing something like passport control. Very serious men, decorated in epaulets with multicaliber stars and even aiguillettes, each with a huge pistol at his hip, began to hand our passports back and forth and with discussion. Evidently, they had learned something quite important about us. After the documents had completed a third circuit, the owner of the largest pistol shoved the passport back into my hands, pointed his finger, said something like "Stamp... stamp..." and motioned with his head back in the direction we'd just come from.

ASKING THE RIGHT QUESTIONS

These stamps, at a cost of twenty American dollars, were glued into the passports of people who were leaving the country, while we were only flying to Aleppo. But there wasn't any time to think about it. To go back and buy two stamps, I had to speak with the security staff at the checkpoint, competing with them in expressive gestures. Not having finished the conversation, I darted over to the counter, explaining to the indignant line something like "Aleppo! Flight! Too late! No time! I'm screwed! Please..." I shoved some money into the window and grabbed my stamps.

And there we were again in front of the three guards, or supreme judges, who were to determine our right to board the precious plane. The boss, with our passports and stamps once more in his hands, turned them over and showed them to his colleagues while the boarding period was coming to an end. And then the truly unexpected happened, and I couldn't believe my eyes...

Some twelve years before this moment, at the very beginning of the '90s, I spent several days in Lviv in western Ukraine. The usual highlight of the tourist program was a visit to the local flea market. Before I went there, my acquaintances gave me some safety tips. A buddy who had rich life experiences shared with me the characteristic techniques for dishonestly handling other people's money and explained that if I were to see anything like this, I ought to grab onto my cash and make noise as loudly as possible. One of these types of tricks was called a "wipe," in which several counted bills were hidden beneath the little and ring finger during the course of calculation.

And right there in nighttime Damascus, I picked up on a familiar movement and understood that they were giving me back the passports—but where were the stamps?! Without even thinking, I grabbed and turned up the tanned wrists... There were our stamps, sticking out from beneath the little finger!

A tableau vivant played out from eye to eye, and an unperturbed officer once again handed back the two passports in a gesture of the illusionist, this time with the stamps already inside. After that, all three of the guards found something unreasonably interesting on the wall somewhere behind and above our heads, making it clear that we no longer existed in their reality.

We still made it to Aleppo, and I got a nice lesson and proof that people from another country are definitely not aliens from another universe.

As my experience demonstrates, falling into our "twilight zone," where the solution to a problem in its correct formulation can be exchanged for a convenient compromise, "special" foreigners quickly adapt and become "the same." I was already familiar with European regulation when I asked an expert from Finland why he took such liberties in technical matters here when, at home, his reputation would suffer tremendously for them. Without giving it a second thought, he gave a comprehensive answer: "We're in Russia."

I had used to consider the Japanese as a certain standard in matters of quality and reliability, but when I myself learned the lessons, it turned out the representatives of the Land of the Rising Sun could be just as cunning as others on occasion. In localized production in Russia, according to the words and pictures in the presentations, everything was done according to Japanese standards, complying with all the principles of Kanban and Kaizen and all other trendy management techniques. Without much effort, however, I was able to find those same familiar tricks in the documentation as were employed by the local "masters of adaptation." The necessary verifications and proofs were also forgotten about, and all that was required was belief in whatever was written on the label.

Our project with a gold mining plant on Kolyma (a very beautiful and very, very cold land in the northeast part of Russia) underwent a technical audit with the participation of Canadian and British experts. The specialist from London persistently pointed out threats and risks and cut our technical solutions to ribbons. He did all this very thoroughly and for no small cost. The expert drew a three-dimensional coordinate system using colored arrows and demanded an answer to the question of how our structure would withstand loads acting in all three directions.

A thank you to a colleague from Manchester who some five years ago straightforwardly explained that when people do not want to disassemble a difficult task into its most basic components, it's likely because they understand it poorly themselves. So, I propose we begin with something simple. Dear expert, the vertical arrow is the force of gravity by which we can calculate and use it to construct a model. But the other two arrows in this three-dimensional system—what part of the physics textbook are these from? Instead of providing a direct response, the expert once again began listing off terrible threats: earthquakes, deformations, and temperature fluctuations, writing about the importance and the difficulty of these threats. What ought the evidence look like to satisfy the expert—a calculation using proven data or an authoritative opinion that brooks no argument? If calculations need to be done, then we'll do them. If something needs to be verified, then we'll verify it. Then the solution will be equally understandable in any language. If not, then we might as well just immediately go ask the Queen of England, since it seems as though we can't get by without her.

As I mentioned, I had a good occasion to understand how the same processes are organized abroad when I managed the Russian branch of an international holding for fourteen years. In general, I was quite lucky in terms of having people I could learn from. It was great being surprised at how my foreign colleague could resolve with the snap of the fingers the question that left me at an impasse. They also helped me to understand what our potential partners could expect from us and what possibilities we could objectively lay out for that purpose. To do that, I'd have to see the problem through their eyes and "walk in their shoes" to understand their logic. This constantly pushed me to obtain knowledge in neighboring areas and didn't give me the chance to start viewing my work as a boring routine. The company had an inexhaustible source of such experience accumulated over decades by truly universal specialists. It was great to then share my own solutions with them and to feel how I had begun to be worth something in the eyes of my teachers.

But the shareholders experienced a changing of the guard: "Grandchildren" came to replace "grandfathers." There were very few "grandfathers" who had built this business and developed it for several decades. There were almost fifty "grandchildren," however, and for the business to live up to their expectations, urgent planning to bring about a decisive success was necessary. Now at each meeting, we did not exchange experience and knowledge but listened to presentations of new strategies with examples, quotes from business gurus, rising graphs, and exciting prospects.

Upon careful consideration, some of the innovations turned out to be already well-known solutions, just presented a bit differently. Another portion of the new ideas was so poorly thought out once it came to details that they required a fair bit of work before they could rush full speed ahead into a "breakthrough."

One of those breakthrough ideas was that, if we are involved in the pipe business, then all the pictures in our booklets and brochures ought to be made round. This way, we'd start influencing our audience at a subconscious level and overtake our unlucky competitors still using square illustrations. It seemed to me that this was appropriate for advertising materials, but for the most part I was writing for specialists. Try conveying technical information using a variety of round spots of various shades and sizes, and my reader will stop taking in the content after just the second page. But my words fell on deaf ears.

As usual, I turned to an older colleague for advice, and this experienced fellow explained, short and sweet: "For us, this is a job, but for them it's a Big Strategy." He suggested I prepare my presentation but advised that, to start, I look at the first row of the "parterre," where leadership and shareholder representatives typically sit and think. Could I create such a convincing compilation following similar templates, quotes, and examples of "successful success," then repeat that exercise every four months at each regular management meeting? It would be better to ignore my real knowledge of the business that looked rather boring despite the good results. The main question was—would they be interested in listening to me? For my colleague and his like, it was simpler, as they were doing a job that they had come to understand, while I would be forced to sell an imitation, over and over again. Could I imagine what sort of stress the performer of such a show experienced each time?

Another attack of *deja vu* came over me at compliance training, which was conducted by a specialist from one of the Big Four of the best and most expensive international auditors. They spent a long time thoroughly explaining what formal indicators were used to identify dubious interactions. Being sorted into the category of "suspicious" would be practically equivalent to the misconduct itself, just like with my familiar experience at Russian customs. To avoid falling into the "risk group," thereby clearing yourself of suspicion, you had to, at the slightest whiff of doubt, contact the Compliance Commissioner.

It was forbidden to spend more than fifty euros per person at restaurants (I most often violated this restriction with the very colleagues who were tasked with ensuring compliance with these requirements), you could not cross paths with a relative at work either, nor could you give gifts, send invitations, or mention certain things in correspondence in both the literal and figurative sense because that can be considered dubious according to some formal approach... The trainer then moved on to skill consolidation—you had to produce quickly the expected answer, without displaying any doubts, such that, like a circus poodle, you could catch the reward tossed your way: candy or some sort of promotional trinket.

A reflex learned during my ten years of managing an independent business unit snapped into action: I began to calculate how much the time of everyone assembled in the meeting hall was worth—we still had to earn that money for the company, after all. Here we all were, gathered together to go over the fact that we operate with large sums. We ought to have been winning contracts away from our competitors, making a profit, and could only be bleeding-heart altruists on our off hours if we wanted. Simultaneously, we all had to appear selfless, like medieval Franciscan monks, and, in addition to that, in order to avoid the slightest suspicion, had to perform all the necessary cleansing rituals for sinners, thereby proving that we were not offenders to the compliance board.

I tried to determine roughly how much an hour of this coach in a toupee and expensive suit, carried away in a frenzy of writing with a variety of colors, cost us, and just what threats they were protecting us from. Judging by the pressure to attend, we were being sold something very expensive. The first "Believe me!" the coach shouted at the very beginning of the session, then repeated it every five to ten minutes. Personally, for me, even the second "Believe...!" was already superfluous. Professional adult human beings (assuming that the audience gathered was such) ought to understand what they're doing, just believing doesn't get them very far.

Some gatekeepers write and modify the general instruction on "how to identify those who seem like criminals." Others interpret this *Malleus Maleficarum* and advise us on what to do to avoid any type of suspicion. Everyone is involved in important business and makes good money for it. Of course, such a compliance procedure also makes life more difficult for villains, but, since they're villains, they find ways to circumvent such obstacles. Moreover, as a result of their previous villainy, they've acquired resources they can use to help them do so. What, then, were we ultimately doing? Solving problems or creating new ones for ourselves?

It seems to me that fairytales about specially manufactured, law-abiding ethnic groups have roughly the same practical significance as the scientific thesis about the direct connection between national mentality and the chemical composition of feces (from the first chapter, in case you forgot). The longer you work with foreign colleagues, the better you understand that they're pretty much the same. The difference is somehow they manage to deceive each other and themselves a little less. Usually, they understand that what depends solely on them and not on others. The moment when they agree to do something simply because "everyone else does it and nothing happens to them" comes later. There's less need to worry that the right formulation may seem disagreeable or turn out to be inconvenient. If the solution to a problem isn't preoccupied with the status of participants or with disputes, with clarifying who is the most important and most correct, then there's a better chance of focusing on the problem itself.

For the most part, their System solves understandable problems as a system of equations, concerning itself with everyone at once and nobody in particular. In comparison with ours, their System recognizes errors a little earlier, and the costs are paid by those who committed them rather than everyone, or whoever the System decides to appoint as the guilty party.

Beyond that, they experience very similar difficulties. A person who understands the meaning and significance of their work quite well has a bad habit of demanding adequate compensation. The attempt to replace this worker comes in the form of a retooled management schema that poses a solution to the problem. If leadership is too fond of creating formalized protocols, then workers will always have to walk the balance beam before the following choice: focus on the task or adapt to the procedure. It's always easier to adapt. This is already familiar to us because of our friend the "goat scholar," who selects the necessary numbers and finds the right names but hardly understands the task itself.

Paradoxically, the assumption itself is that the deployment of ready-made success formulas, seasoned with convincing examples, is enough to beat out competitors. Almost all the participants in this competition are reading and listening to practically the same thing. Managers show how many ready-made solutions they've learned by rote or spied on from each other and how little free space is left in their heads for their own research. An honorable mention must go to the art of explaining your own failures and selling them as "a near thing." How can you break forward just by copying the movements of other people, doing the exact same thing that the vast majority are doing?

The knowledge of others and ready-made schemas are quite useful, but only your own research grants you the possibility of real success. Without that, without an attempt to understand what you're doing, it all comes down to a zero-sum game. You can quote distinguished geniuses and champions, but the principal difference between the author and those who repeat their words remains and keeps you swimming in place. At some point, the author has to think for themselves rather than copy down something already written.

We converge in the desire to grab onto the ready-made and convenient "truth" instead of conducting our own search so as to avoid pushing ourselves too hard, hiding our uncertainty behind false confidence. Real confidence can only be found by understanding in-depth your field of employment. It's replaced by other people's thoughts, schemas, templates, and ready-made recipes for success. These thoughts don't need to be examined, no further searching needs to be done, and you needn't take responsibility for the results of your personal decisions. If all ideas are secondary, then all that remains is suggestion and faith, exercises in collective hysteria at large events, no different from gatherings of religious sects and having nothing in common with movement towards the present goal. Even the successful "thoughts of others" have ceased to be used as tools; we rather grab at them like crutches and are unable to let go of them when it's time for us to walk on our own. In the schema or model invented by one person but accepted by the majority as truth, there will always be flaws and assumptions that will eventually break off from reality. Someone will always try to use this to extract additional benefits at the expense of less sophisticated participants.

Individual, personal effort is a necessary condition for any type of conscious and directed movement. No mentor and no ready-made schema can take my place to look at my problem and find a resolution for me. If another person does so, they're taking my opportunities along with my money.

In some ways, we're still different. For example, we believe our own make-believe stories to varying degrees. And these stories are different for each of us. Nonetheless, we do believe them, because we're human and, this way, it's easier for us to get through the day.

~ CHAPTER FIFTEEN ~
SO-SO PROSPECTS

By the way, about fairytales. Futurological forecasts that now resound every which way argue that very soon the System will consider a significant portion of humanity (that is, us) practically useless. Everywhere, wherever possible, robots and algorithms will come to take the place of people. According to the most daring assumptions, human beings will reproduce via test tube and satisfy their sexual appetites in virtual reality. Those so shortchanged, who already believe that the strongest and most striking feelings can be experienced via electronic gadgets, simply lack the courage and imagination to pursue a connection with another real person. If humanity really does go the electronics and test tube route, then for some reason I don't feel so terrible if a civilization of such principled masturbators slowly dies off. I won't risk delving deeper into such dangerous waters. It's reasonable to suggest that if the System, created and operated by human beings, is not able to lead to a better solution, that means there is something wrong with the System itself. So, let's fight for our place in the economy instead of being scared and admitting our helplessness.

It's amazing how easily amongst the tricks and miracles the computer produces the real inventor—human beings—can be completely lost. In the ancient '80s, a printout of the *Mona Lisa*, made on the first stylus printers, became quite popular. These printers could produce lines and a limited set of symbols, but someone went to the trouble of creating this fashionable image at their serious, boring job. The audience only saw the result—the "computer *Mona Lisa*," while those who "painted" it saw just a stack of perforated cards, two hefty, rumbling metal boxes, and a kick in the pants from management for "taking out the paper and getting into all kinds of nonsense while on the job." We're impressed by the fact of the output (look, like that picture, the machine really made the *Mona Lisa*!) and overlook the actual creator. Also, in another case, when our greatest masters lose to the computer, then we ought to broaden our gaze and see that, in fact, the chess player is competing with a whole host of intelligent people who spent more than a week pumping their machine full of their own and other people's knowledge with the help of code.

In order for another "deus ex machina" to be born, the program must refrain from making mistakes for a certain period of time and its result ought to live up to our expectations enough for us to shift responsibility over to it, stop thinking for ourselves, understanding, and keeping our eyes open. Pay attention to this trick: Computer calculation or an action when a human uses hardware and software tools, provided by other human beings, begins to exist independently, in complete separation from its actual author. That makes the algorithm yet another "being of a higher order." We believe more in someone else's computer model than in what our own eyes perceive, forgetting that the model was written by someone in another time and another place. No single model can fully reflect reality, its possibilities are limited in the same manner that the information available to its author was limited at the moment of its creation. For a given period, the model will produce the correct solution a hundred times. But your case might be the one hundred and first.

I had such a case when I argued static calculation with the above-mentioned British technical auditor. A British expert used a popular computer program based on the American AWWA method and got a negative result. That was enough to declare all of the project a complete failure. Actually, the American method is a perfect tool for the calculation of standard cases such as a pipe in a trench with a depth of less than ten meters, but we designed a pipe under a dam fifty meters high. For such a specific case, more sophisticated tools like models based on the final element are needed. That was a good demonstration of the familiar approach when we accept a result of a known computer program as the final version of the truth without understanding how this tool actually works in a human's hand.

Certain exquisite algorithms will soon start managing our lives if we've already forgotten that any algorithm is first written by a person—either out of curiosity or ambition, or rather because another person paid for it. The all-powerful algorithm already has one decisive advantage over people. It cannot be asked that sacred question that we usually ask humans: "Why the hell did you do that?" The result of any program must be interpreted by a professional who can understand the issue, take responsibility for the result, and... get paid for their expertise. Good remark for anybody who is too eager about the usage of ChatGPT.

Now, about our inevitable defeat in the competition with high-performance robots. Periodically, lists are published ticking off "dying" professions for which, by tomorrow, there will be no demand. All those who find themselves on the outside of this fundamental engine of progress simply do not have a future. The only chance is to digitize or get closer to any sort of electronic gadget. But here's the rub: Clearly, there isn't enough space for everyone in this digital paradise.

All that remains is for us to descend, as if in a trance, directly into a gloomy fairytale, like something out of the series *Black Mirror*. In one episode from the first season, people have ceased to be engaged in production, instead just pedaling on stationary bikes to generate energy; evidently, human beings are no longer useful for anything. But this isn't even rock bottom—the real unlucky ones clean up the garbage of those who do the pedaling. Everyone lives in these multimedia capsules, dressed exactly the same and getting their food from vending machines, which they pay to use the money they earn from "pedaling." Their remaining funds can be used to purchase the personalized media content of their choice. If you pedal badly, then you'll simply watch whatever's shown to you. For a lot of money, you can try your chance at happiness and ascending to the rank of the Chosen Few, those people who are displayed on the monitors. To do this, you have to be able to attract attention to yourself and maintain it for as long as possible.

We've almost swallowed hook, line, and sinker that the

proliferation of robots is inevitable, a practically natural process, forgetting that, apart from people no one else is a participant in this game. Let's get this straight: A person cannot lose to a robot for the simple fact that the robot is not competing with them. The robot is not a participant or a player at all—it doesn't have motives, goals, or desires. The real player is another person. They are using new technological capabilities to further their interests, not paying attention to the consequences for the rest, and redrawing the System to suit them. Conversations about the inexorability of technological progress are either a clever trick or else an attempt to give a pseudoscientific justification for something they don't want to fully admit.

We're used to measuring a person's economic significance by the yardstick of their money. Okay, what about people with incomes below average which represented the vast majority and suggested here as least significant? Gradually we'll write them off as ballast and transfer them to capsules. A large number of resources in the hands of a single person is not, however, the achievement of this *Forbes* champion alone. Rather, they accumulate the results of a multitude of less significant operations. If there are no "trivialities," then billionaire status doesn't exist. The successes of any product are determined by the number of people who manage to buy it because the buyer is a necessary part of any economic transaction. It is no one but another person who needs offered staff, and this person has to offer something useful for other people in response. Jeff Bezos and Jack Ma didn't make their money solely by interacting with bankers and programmers. The main source of their capital is the potentially useless mass. If we stop valuing this mass of low-income people, then soon enough the majority of billionaires will cease to exist. Don't you think that the category of "useless," from the perspective of the robotic and high-performance System, will eventually come to encompass today's futurologists, too? Economists and financiers, masters of today's internet trading sites—of what use will they be when the economy as such no longer exists for the vast majority of people in the world? That's right—we'll all be pedaling together. How smart you are!

It looks like we keep the tool to balance the System in our hands, but we use it like monkeys. Even if we lose to robots as manufacturers, there's no way we can lose to them as buyers so long as the laws of economics are in effect. Robotic production only pays off on a large scale, at the level of production of a mass, serial product. The post-apocalyptic villain commanding an army of robots won't be able to achieve dangerous levels of power if there isn't anyone to buy their product at the necessary volume. If that's so, then they simply will not be able to rebuild the System according to their whim, waving the flag of technological progress and the common good.

No one is thrusting us into this gloomy apocalypse but ourselves. Certainly not robots or algorithms, just people who don't want to understand how best to use their new capabilities without shooting themselves in the foot. People won't lose to artificial intelligence either. The person who gives up now is simply capitulating before their own invention, without even waiting for the machine to start interpreting information and writing its own programs. For now, we're talking about a certain character who very much wants to make use of these new opportunities but doesn't want to answer for the consequences, concocting a smokescreen of smart words to shield themselves from responsibility.

For starters, we have to admit that we're not dealing with "irreversible technological progress," as unruly and ungovernable as a seismic shift. Throughout its history, humankind has discovered new things and has not immediately been able to understand how to use them. Somehow, we've found a balance between the necessity of using pesticides in agriculture and the unconditional danger of being poisoned by those very same chemicals. I propose we take as a basis the schema that has been in effect already for some millennia, from the moment someone first exchanged a piece of meat for a couple of flint tips for a spear. In this schema, the only real actor is a human being—they are both the producer and the end buyer of any product. We simply must find a solution that allows us to balance the interests and appetites of individual participants such that our general result doesn't decrease in the foreseeable future. That result demonstrates how many times people have found opportunities to do something worthwhile for each other, and it's not so important what that thing is—a car, a bottle of milk, dance lessons, anything that represents value to another person. I'm not proposing we reject robots and computers, but rather that we not lose sight of the fact that these are only tools, and that we should configure our System in such a way that it doesn't eliminate active people as unnecessary, instead retaining the ability for them to convert an hour of their life into something useful. We need to fight for that chance, making sure our work is, at minimum, of average quality, and some people still don't have the ability, motivation, or just good luck. People find work for each other and set common goals for which they never find decisive solutions. If earlier a set of tools and knowledge could be passed from generation to generation and still retain its value, now the emphasis must be placed on learning capability, on the ability to change and rebuild their own skillsets under changing conditions and at the requests of others. In such a setting, the task, at the very least, has a solution, and the tragedy of the untalented majority stretches far past the horizon.

Discussion of values is yet another game that a human plays on themselves. The real value of any item is determined by the readiness of someone to give something in exchange for it. We create something that represents value for a unit of time—this is the speed at which we live. Then we ourselves must buy what we've created, since there's no one else who will. Unless we teach dolphins to jump for money instead of fish. In the end, we have to hand over the hours of our lives, spent first on the acquisition of knowledge and skills, then on work itself. Those who have already achieved a good speed, which is measured by incomes per unit of time or GDP per year, must take into account the System's stability and drivability before zooming ahead. Especially in those moments when turns must be taken, reacting to changing circumstances and man-made crises. We really believe that our speed should accelerate at any cost, measuring this growth in terms of goods made and sold which have ended up in the garbage dump faster and faster. Is it possible that we judge something worthy simply out of inertia? If we're talking about values, then it's high time we ask ourselves the question: What do we value? Do we do this consciously or are we unconsciously complying with familiar conventions?

Once, at subarctic Kolyma, I was looking into a giant pit left at the foot of a mountain under which they had found gold. The times of the conquistadors, prospectors, and "gold fever" have long passed. We live in the 21st century and our techniques allow us to process a million tons of ore per month at even just one enterprise. Unlike other useful minerals, half of the gold mined isn't used in any way. It's only mined to place ingots in a safe and demonstrate wealth, so long as the majority of people believe that it's true.

With the invention of the loan, we learned to sell our chances in the foreseeable future to realize our capabilities and time on the market. Taking out a loan is like selling a piece of one's time—a couple of months or several weeks each following year to repay the debt. But now, in addition to "real" obligations secured by the hours of someone's life, markets are dominated by liabilities and promises that no one plans to fulfill completely, such as public debts or valuable papers which suggested to be paid by selling new pledges. They're not reviewed so long as the curve on the graph turns upward in accordance with the forecasts. If the curve takes a sharp turn, part of the financial bubble bursts, taking a portion of the income and savings of real people with it. Even without these sharp fluctuations, the money of real people gradually dissipates due to the inflation that follows this make-believe growth. Players find new ways to pawn their own futures and those of others, convincing both themselves and others that tomorrow there'll definitely be a spike, and due to that spike, it'll be possible to pay down accumulated interest and make new bets. Even if you don't wish to participate in this casino, someone else will still put your money in it. A person trying to do something other people need loses to those who can take on debts they never have to pay back.

At a 2019 investment forum, novice financiers gathered, all as one, tomorrow's "money masters." One of the presenters decided, for some reason, to let down their hair. This really big trader tried explaining to the audience that, basically, they are food. Firstly, for those not in this room, who are waiting for these hungry and ambitious beginners to come and bring with them the money of those who believed there was a short and sweet way of becoming rich without getting up from the couch. Later, those gathered in the hall would eat each other, and only a few of them would have the chance to come out solidly on top.

Only one person would hit the jackpot, or, maybe, a few finalists. But the jackpot is just the money of less successful players. The speaker talked, but I hardly assumed that many of the listeners in the room believed him. Everyone thought this trader was being clever, guarding his secrets, his gold mine. But all of them were motivated, armed with the best and practically identical programs, they would manage to guess, would find...

Cowrie shells of a certain shape were once used as money. In the past, somewhere in the Pacific Ocean, not just for shells, you could buy lots of useful things—fish, for example. What might have happened if the masses had stopped catching fish and rushed to collect shells instead? More likely than not, we would have seen a lot of "rich" but hungry people. Something like this is currently happening with our System, which we've so overloaded with tired, ready-made forms that we've stopped understanding what it is we've created. It's helping some people to further exploit the System's shortcomings in pursuit of their own benefit, unconsciously bringing closer the moment when all these accumulated riches will turn to dust.

~ CHAPTER SIXTEEN ~
A LOSS OF MEANING

Ready-made answers—thoughts that don't require further consideration—distract from questions in the correct formulation that help you to find the necessary solutions. They're constantly on offer, and even imposed very aggressively. We don't have time to ask: How long did the authors themselves spend thinking about this? Or did they just do the same as we do—pull suitable fragments from a huge mass of incoming information and quickly glue together something convincing and similar in form to the truth?

The forecasts about which we spoke in the last chapter aren't presented to us today by science fiction writers. Rather, they come from the mouths of people with academic titles, meaning that we ought to be able to trust them. I'll call such authors "academicians" and take this word with a grain of salt. This sort of "academician" is what you get when a real scientist acts in the same manner as the large majority of us by taking the path of least resistance and not conducting actual research. Their task is to give a very convincing explanation of what's going on with some pretension of originality. I understand why. They have to be published, perform, build up their citation index, collect honoraria, earn invitations to conferences and a place in the Academy.

A popular trick is extracting suitable, vivid fragments from a whole picture or historical context and using them to compile proof of a new version of the truth. In *Why Nations Fail: The Origins of Power, Prosperity, and Poverty* by Daron Acemoglu and

James A. Robinson, the authors produce a plain conclusion about the fall of medieval Venice—Venice succeeded with inclusive institutes based on democracy and failed as far as the power was concentrated among the high nobility. There's no mention, however, of the rivalry and conflicts between Venice and Byzantium that led to the alliance with participants of the Fourth Crusade and the role of Venetians in the destruction of Constantinople. Not one word about how the Ottoman Empire appeared nearby and changed the situation completely. No mention of the Era of Maritime Discoveries that drew main trade routes across oceans and left Venice in the backyard of world trade. Just plain conclusion—all losses of Venice happened because the institutes became more extractive.

Examples and citations from the works of recognized geniuses and Nobel laureates lend persuasiveness to their arguments. The authors, along with their grateful audience, lose sight of the fact that these references are no longer reliable truths but simply clues in an investigation. Rather than asking questions, however, the academician earns more money and applause by providing complete, convincing answers for yet another thousand buzzwords proving that water is, indeed, wet.

What is happening comes across as a competition of abstract descriptions, each one pretending to be the most accurate. Liberalism with authoritarianism, socialism with capitalism, the market with the centrally planned economy—empty forms fighting with each other, people trying to appoint one among them as the winner.

In practice, those who achieve a good overall economic result don't shy away from the use of capitalism. Capitalism is nothing but an effective scheme to construct economic interaction based on large-scale industrial capital goods. Then they raise the level of social security, attracting the state to this task. They've received enough resources, kept the number of people on the margins to a minimum, and established a management apparatus to justify expenses—they have a decent level of social protection, which, for some reason, is presented as a triumph of socialism. But where, exactly, is the triumph or defeat of an abstract idea here—the capitalism in a vision of Karl Marx or the socialism of the '70s and '80s of the last century? How do we remember it? I described how we copied templates of market economics and applied them with a lot of mistakes in the former Soviet Union. These changes were quite painful and chaotic, but we blame liberal ideas for poor performance and disappointment with the result. What will we do—keep arguing about which of these alternative constructions is better, or allow that neither is a ready-made answer but just a tool?

It's foolish to argue about some final verdict, some final version of the best System. The situation is constantly changing, and a balance must be found to decide on the system of equations into which life is always throwing new values and variables. Ideals and frightening images are of little help in this. Showy phrases about how one kind any abstract idea has died off, while another, on the other hand, has proven its claims that unconditional truth doesn't make any particular sense. It's just a matter of intelligent words being bandied about by unintelligent people who just provoke an emotional response but do not bother to understand the meaning.

Behind the verbosity hides an inability or unwillingness to understand. It's more interesting to sniff at, weigh, listen to, and shake the "black box," selecting and sticking different labels on it designed to explain, according to their authors, what's inside. One must choose the correct definitions from the bottomless reserve created by one's predecessors and, with the help of these labels, lend the appearance of an exhaustive explanation. The trouble is that the authors don't want to see beyond these labels and have no desire to as far as it fits their logic.

If we're talking about an economy in which there are no subjects besides people, then we can easily open the lid. It's all very simple. Each of us is the same "sapiens" as the researchers themselves. There's no need for modeling them, for harping on all their weaknesses, instincts left over from their primate ancestors. They can instead be presented with a conscious choice. Imagining current events as a result of incomprehensible processes that can only be modeled and described, and viewing reasonable human beings as "black boxes" is a very convenient excuse for avoiding responsibility for the inevitable mistakes and losses. A permanent manmade crisis of modern economic institutes in this instance is nothing more than a logical result.

The academicians' abstract constructions are good in that one can always find in them something suitable as a ready-made answer. The thought that they "stopped thinking" approaches the next stage, the most interesting one, and with its help, they begin to designate who is right and who is guilty. The "Pied Pipers" are connected to this process, like in the fairy tale about the rats of Hamelin town.

The "Pied Piper" has a slightly different task; now, we're moving from purely scientific research directly to politics. In principle, the Piper acts in exactly the same manner as the academician. They select and paste together from informational fragments something that seems logical and convincing, except their task is to cause an emotional reaction of the desired type. Logic, as with the veracity of what is said, doesn't play a big role here. Rather, the Piper's product is designed to have a time-limited effect. The Piper assigns the roles, setting up one party as the definition of guilt when it comes to the current issue, and another as the incarnation of hope for its resolution. They will never get bogged down in unprofitable details and, in response to any inconvenient questions, they will lean on the emotional appeal. They'll go from a low, ominous rumble to a squeal, using examples, quotes, and industrial-grade air fresheners to beat back the stench. And it will stink because, from the perspective of our actual tasks, all these constructions are rotten products—we're just going further and further away from real decision-making. Their primary efforts are directed at manipulating human weaknesses, not at all towards taking conscious steps in pursuit of common goals. The version of the truth proffered up by the Piper has very little in common with solutions to problems. An urgent and painful challenge is just a formal excuse for performance. Most important of all is neither the formulation of questions nor their answers. The main thing is speculation over subjects causing painful responses. People's emotional reactions are the real goal.

Then, there's the unequivocal division of things into "black" and "white," into those who are "for" and those who are "against." Proposals to clarify and think things through no longer have any sway; they'll be trampled on and shouted over by both sides because the "Drummers" have entered the show.

If the Piper must string together some kind of coherent and logical sequence, then the Drummer needs only a familiar phrase to react. The simple way of pushing a person to an irrational act is to go after the primate sitting inside everyone—just lure it out with bright light and the scent of food, scare it, and direct it with a painful charge or images of threats The opportunity to voice a question of substance and return to the topic of discussion is irrevocably lost—the Drummer cannot and doesn't want to hear about this. They react to words and images the way Pavlov's dog did with a lightbulb: In certain instances, they choke on their own hysterical barking, while in others they wag their tail for "food" and yelp joyfully. The Drummers also know all the words and utter them in "suitable" combinations, obviously disagreeing with anything "unsuitable." For them, there exists a simple and understandable dividing line between "friend" and "foe," between the right and the guilty, depending on the reaction to their own version of the truth. Beyond the singularly correct formula, there's nothing inside them like inside a drum. The volume of sound depends on how empty they really are.

Like the Piper, the Drummer only needs a common problem as an excuse. Therefore, the realization of everything they've promised or declared is the last thing one should expect here. The link between whoever it is who seems guilty and the problem on that day's agenda is already a given for them, regardless of the truth. The need to prove and calculate practical steps or evaluate their own mistakes lies beyond the parameters of discussion. In response to such requests, the Drummer simply turns the volume up to eleven. In the most critical cases, they'll bring on an attack of righteous anger, start foaming at the mouth, and fall into a seizure.

The side the speaker takes in the course of the discussion is no longer relevant because the antagonists are both fulfilling a role in the same farce. The audience is waiting for catharsis, but it never comes because the very thought of real answers or real changes in this instance is absurd. These are words spoken not so much in order to formulate and convey a real thought or to share someone's own experience. These are words spoken to get money or to provoke emotion cynically. They might be evocative but empty phrases pronounced for the simple reason of maintaining the author's status, as they need to periodically say something smart. They might be intriguing compilations stitched together from bright fragments, attempting to give off an impression of deep meaning. Reality is hidden behind these flat, bright pictures that we sheepishly call "post-truth." It's an appropriate label for the expensive, synthetic product of the Pipers, for the deafening hooch of the Drummers, and the breezy, brain-melting weed of the academicians.

Here is where everyone gathers who is lost in the current of other people's thoughts, arguments that no longer need to be pondered because they're all "right." This sort of listener obtains an illusion of security, the understanding of what awaits them tomorrow, the feeling that they, and those they're listening to, are right. They accept the truth that suits them better so as not to have to think for themselves and take responsibility for their own choices. Here, next to their version of the truth, everyone who is gathered here is safe and will be rewarded. Everything bad and dangerous, the reason for all the problems, is somewhere out there, by another idol, where a hostile and no less confused crowd has amassed.

There's a type of fishing bait known as a caddis worm that, in my childhood, we called a "*shitik*." It lives in shallow water and glues together, out of garbage that has sunk to the water's floor, a protective case for itself that guards against fish. But this "armor" crumbles easily, even from the touch of a child's fingers, and although the *shitik* desperately digs in its heels, it ends up on a fishing hook, nonetheless.

Our grateful listener constructs approximately the same type of protection for themselves from all those slogans, promises, and explanations. While they're inside, surrounded by like-minded people, drawing their ideas about righteousness from the same source, they feel confident, no matter what they do. They'll never abandon their "fortress" and will defend themselves and kick up as much of a fuss as they can muster.

There is no real movement. When the break with those who haven't lost themselves in a bunch of dead truths, who have thought and moved forward, becomes too obvious, those disappointed seekers of righteousness might be able to change their words and rituals, but not their modus operandi. Chronically shell-shocked, pockets emptied out, they'll go to another idol to get their allotment of confidence and ready-made answers. In order to make a simple choice, they need to know which idol to bless and in what direction they must send curses to ensure we have success in business and good weather. It can't be otherwise, because they stake their bets on their own weakness, on their grievances, fears, and empty hopes. Their hero needs only to play the role convincingly. Such a leader doesn't have anything to say to strong people capable of making a conscious choice or sharing responsibility for their consequences, having no need to hide in a protective bubble on which is written the words "I'm right, and you're all lyyyiiinngg...."

Before giving up and jumping to conclusions about the inability of the majority to conduct themselves rationally, I propose we include for consideration the manipulators themselves—those who push others to irrational acts. Then the behavior of the entire group becomes predictable, as the manipulators are entirely pragmatic. Whatever truthers are broadcast on the airwaves, they will, as a result, share money and votes, leaving a little for the idealists.

The strangest of characters can succeed as populists and make their way to the uppermost positions in the System if they can provoke emotional reactions better than others without offering meaningful action. They even have the chance to improve the System slightly, forcing you to examine many questions from new angles. This happens only if the System is well-balanced, and the populist is limited in their ability to direct things using the argument of "That's how it should be" in lieu of providing exhaustive evidence.

It's necessary to find some way to drown out the feeling of cognitive dissonance and to fill in the gaps between their reality and the fanciful imagery. To do this, the media must constantly generate more words that are easier to sell. They have to "try out" more, find a nerve that has not yet stopped reacting in order to pull on it once again, like a string.

Not everyone can ask a correctly formulated right question, and even fewer want to answer one. Difficult and inconvenient, this question will render a protective shell, pieced together from righteousness and false confidence, into dust. It will tear apart the chain of academic compilations, expose the false note in the Piper's interpretations, and be heard even above the roar of the Drummers.

Think that seems harsh and a bit like misanthropy? Not at all. Don't rush to interrupt an unpleasant conversation. Yes, it'll be easier that way, but it's worth seeing what might grow from the "right" thoughts that no longer need to be thought, and what dangerous toxins are produced in this environment.

~ CHAPTER SEVENTEEN ~
GHASTLY TALES

In Andalusia, there is an amazing place—Ronda. Many people know it from the photos of the New Bridge, or *Puente Nuevo*, that has stretched across the abyss since the 18th century. This is a place where you can literally see history, look into the past, like into a well. Everyone left a tangible mark here: the Romans, the Goths, the Saracens, the Crusaders. They liked this natural fortress—a city on a cliff, surrounded on three sides by an impregnable chasm. Hemingway liked it here, too. It seems that here he left another mark, as if he'd slashed the canvas with a piercing razor. A shiver runs down your spine when you look into this gash—the tenth chapter of *For Whom the Bell Tolls*.

The very beginning of the Civil War was the moment when the killing started. A man with a flail in his hands must hit another and then find a reason for doing so. The executioners consider themselves republicans and know that people like them have already been killed in neighboring towns, so here they decide to strike first. The victims have not yet done anything to their killers, and all their fault so far lies in the fact that they recently began to call themselves fascists. This is the very beginning—the middle of the 1930s, so do not rush to react so painfully to the word *fascist*. It is better to reread this brilliant story about the first day of the revolution in the small town atop the high cliff.

It may have been yesterday that you read Hemingway or watched *Hotel Rwanda* and worried about the hero, played by Don Cheadle, but those were stories about Spaniards, Tutsis and

Hutus, Serbs and Croatians, Jews, and Arabs—about other peoples who lived in another time and another country. Until recently, these conflicts all made for a good story, but, over and over again, similar events repeat themselves closer and closer to home. Today, you are sometimes forced to make a choice, and this is no longer a film or a novel. Next to you, they begin to oppress and kill just to answer a very important question—which people will now say "That is how it should be" in a certain territory, by what criteria will they be classified as "right" or "wrong"? It is obvious that for the "us" and the "them" the real problems will remain where they've always been, they cannot be solved by changing the flag, rhetoric, or state language. Therefore, both sides lose in the end.

It looks like everybody speaks the right words and does the right things. But if not today, then tomorrow, you yourself will be one step away from hitting another one, despite both of you having never seen each other before. Or you will stand with your shoulders scrunched to your ears, waiting for a hit yourself because your neighbor realized that you were his new enemy yesterday. And it will push you closer to the cliff, and the stone jaws on the bottom of the abyss will fly up to meet you with a crunch, bite, and a flash of extraordinary pain. And another chasm, another hungry maw will open up somewhere else and wait for the one who pushed you.

Each side of any such conflict repeats the same words about freedom, justice, and independence, and is ready to defend them all from attack. The nature of any kind of such conflict is a mess between neighbors. Moreover, half have relatives and friends on both sides, but if you follow the general criteria, they are the new enemy. You can call this enemy on the phone, even meet and talk—but then this story is not about us, but about someone else. No, as soon as the conversation turns to legality, historical truth, and sovereignty— those things that the disputants represent only in general terms—there are immediate grounds for accusations. Wars and upheavals have always ended with the winners redrawing and recoloring the maps, determining who controls the territories along with the people living on them. As well as they could, they drew, sometimes no better or worse than Pope Borgia, who divided the Atlantic Ocean 500 years ago. Not a single one of those lines was drawn absolutely objectively or fairly, because they were drawn by people who at the time were strongest or turned out to be more sophisticated politicians.

There's always a losing side that is unlikely to agree with their opponents.

I see no fundamental differences between any border lines that were drawn across Africa, Europe, or Asia. It's hard to say anything better about these borders than the Representative of Kenya U.N. Martin in February 2022. He said, as far as we try to define by force which ethnic group, cultural identity, or political doctrine will dominate within certain state borders, there is no solution.

Yesterday's empires, such as the Ottoman, the British Raj in India, or the Soviet Union, lack the heavy tactics to keep control because many factors change the world every day. Administrative conditional borders become official state frontiers in a day, with barbed wire and armed men ready to shoot from both sides. Once, these lines were the solution to the problem, but now they have become another log to add to the fire of the fight.

The main value and necessity of these borders is that today they reflect the conditions under which people stopped killing each other before. Within these boundaries, somebody claims to be a rebel against the System, promising to install the best version with all the latest updates. Others are sure that nothing good will come of this and are ready to defend what is already there. Concerned neighbors intervene to help one of the parties in the conflict—solely for the sake of the triumph of truth and entirely selflessly (the real price will be revealed when the dust settles, and it becomes clear how the assets and power are divided). To correct the injustices of a few aggravated months, a new demolition derby with tanks is urgently needed. Those who do not fit into this model of a "new better world" will be automatically entered in the column of "permissible expenses."

All the nice abstract concepts like freedom, sovereignty, or national interests became nothing but markers to define "friend or foe" in the never-ending fight for domination because each side has its own concept of this. The fight never ended because we have continued this war since the time our ancestors walked on all fours. We define enemies and allies by their reaction to key phrases, and we distribute indulgences to all of our "friends" justifying any of their actions against "foes." Feelings directed at something abstract are distributed among people according to the residual principle. The ability to empathize with fellow believers is more than compensated by the rejection of all who disagree. Even on one side, emotions are not directed at people, but are wasted on common, collective stimuli. The more importance is attached to the discussion of abstract ideas and round dances around common shrines, the less is left for simple empathy between members of the groups, and the less chance that another human being will be seen in the opponent or any dissent. A cause of conflict could be some gesture that people will give unexpectedly significant symbolic meaning.

On June 20, 2019, a terrible thing happened: A representative of the Russian State Duma, following the protocol of this meeting, sat down for a while in the seat of the chairman of the Georgian parliament. Street riots of outraged Georgians followed; direct flights between the countries were severed, and thousands of narrow-minded people tried for several more months to ruin life for themselves and each other. No one voiced a simple solution—to offer the three most offended Georgians their choice of any three seats in Moscow. Not for long—for an hour or two. Let them sit, take a selfie, and boast of a decisive victory. One problem is that there is too much of the public in both countries for whom the fact that the wrong ass is sat briefly in the wrong chair will be more important than healthy relationships between millions of people.

Everybody tries to gain a sense of security—an illusion that everything will be fine because they chose the right side. This confidence is fueled by the number of people around who react the same way to the same words. The more of them there are and the louder they shout, the stronger the feeling of being right. The potential enemies, in the meantime, go about their business, not realizing that they are attacking, occupying, and oppressing someone right now, or they can just as easily be fired up by the rituals of their own shamans and also determined to defeat someone.

Many words will be said about unity, but at the same time, the speakers themselves will tear their own nation apart, dividing people into "us" and "them," referring to their own catechism.

The list of "all that is holy"—which now must be protected at any cost—will be replenished with new applications and interpretations. Victorious fighters for freedom or human dignity first of all find it necessary to bring opponents to their knees.

It is obvious that the 20th century left a lot of traces of human tragedies. True perpetrators are buried, and it does not matter much if they have been declared as winners or losers. People who fail to frankly face their present look for explanations in the past. Instead of focusing on their actual problems, they look for somebody to blame. I cannot find a better explanation for the addiction to the compilation of modern national ideas in the Western parts of the collapsed Soviet Union. Actually, it is nothing but a formal reason to hate ethnic groups based on simplified interpretations of various historical facts mixed with fiction and primitive stereotypes. Nevertheless, such a stupid and dubious distraction step by step became a part of public policy practiced by populists and radicals from all sides. The author of assumptions that justify humiliation and violence against an "alien" is themselves a carrier of a dangerous infection, regardless of their position in society, religion, or other secondary attributes. The danger of infection can arise everywhere: at a sermon, televised debates, or at a parliamentary meeting.

A hastily synthesized version of the truth doesn't stand up to any rational thought and infects the most malleable like a virus, turning them into a herd of bipeds, united by the common idea of being right. They quickly mutate, acquire paraphernalia, choose their own uniforms, and become especially delighted when they gather in very large groups of the same radicals. They train on the graves and monuments of those people who were "in the wrong," leaving evidence of their own wretchedness on each defiled symbol, starting with throwing dirt, insults, and piss jars, and moving on to machine guns and tactical missiles.

The bipeds took the path of least resistance—they chose the most convenient ready-made answers, the simplest rules that help divide their flat monochrome world into the right and the guilty, in order to get rid of the need to ask even one question to themselves today. Each two-legged creature is sure that they are right, and no longer feels for someone else's pain. They scream loudly and heart-wrenchingly, strike frightening poses, and are afraid—they're afraid of sobering up, afraid of the moment when they have to return from this war and find out the real price of their victories. They won't be able to admit that in this war they've already lost, regardless of their chosen side—they lost the fight with their fears and their own insecurities. Step by step, we came to the situation when an aging psychopath decided to play the great leader and made another fatal decision to launch a real war instead of a virtual one.

In terms of losses, this battle for "the greater good" is the most terrible. A biped will do what an animal will never. An animal or even a cannibal can't eat more than their body will allow and so will stop killing. A one-sided and simple version of the truth acceptable to bipeds is that this man-made chimera will devour everything thrown at it and ask for more. This is a war that cannot be won and cannot be ended as long as people continue to find new ways to deceive themselves.

Specially selected and trained characters at summits, forums, and assemblies speak the same abstract words about encroachment on something sacred, dump accusations, and point fingers at one another. Some call one and the same subject freedom fighters, while others call them separatists. In the course of one discussion, one person could be named either a bloody tyrant or the only legitimate guarantor of stability. There is a play on words, and in the meantime, someone is trying to determine through trial and error how many liters of human blood various options for being right can cost. This is no longer a discussion or even a fully-fledged conversation between people—the speakers take turns performing each of their solo numbers for their audience or customers. This doesn't help in any way to progress in resolving the real conflict. Rather, on the contrary, new excuses and new reasons only help to launch a new round of nightmares. I'm not talking about the complete uselessness of such meetings—any platform for discussion is better than a place for a fight, but the only thing speakers ultimately prove is that the problem in this formulation has no solution.

Once a serious conversation has begun, then it's time to quote one of the "greats." Musician and writer Nick Cave and his song "Jubilee Street" will fit.

> *All those good people down on Jubilee Street*
> *They ought to practice what they preach.*

ASKING THE RIGHT QUESTIONS

Yeah, they ought to practice just what they preach…

No one knows who Nick Cave saw in the depths of his own ocean, but he suggested a good formula. Yes, all these good people should practice everything that they so passionately preach.

As far as we use beliefs as a reason to fight so easily, then why not look at a nice general concept as a kind of practical task? To do this, it is necessary to understand, and preferably in detail, what we must do step by step, how, and what will be required to implement such a brilliant idea. Then see what we actually have. If we start to act, we ought to do it step by step, maintaining the ability to correct our thoughts about the ideal in a timely manner and to understand how much it will cost for all participants, and if the losses can be recuperated by the desired result. We need schemas and tools to help us think and understand, to create algorithms to solve problems.

As soon as any idea or assumption is declared to be an indisputable truth and claims to be the only correct and undoubted one, the process of its degradation begins. A minute ago, it was an attempt to take a step towards solving the problem, and now this idea is turning into an empty slogan or a battle cry. It no longer carries any thought and only helps those who share this idea to identify their own as a certain side of the handmade conflict. These are no longer words that carry meaning, this is the scream of an aggressive primate, ready to attack.

Let's say that the countries with developed democracies show the most impressive economic successes (again, an authoritarian regime, as a rule, shows good growth only from a "low base"). Another plus of parliamentarism is that maintaining order requires less violence and coercion.

But is it worth it to build immediately a copy of the Bundestag or Westminster somewhere in Libya or Somalia and expect that European recipes for success will achieve the desired result? Certain conditions are specific all the time. If you really want to build anything, then you have to mean it. If you play some new crusader, better stay home. As at any construction site, let's begin with geological surveys—let's remember all the significant conflicts in this territory, at least over the past one hundred years (or better, two hundred). These are gaps or mines in the foundation of our structure that should not be ignored. We look closely at the material: At people, at the nature of their relationship with each other. You should not count on stable ties that work on general principles where the representative of the dominant cult or the leader of the tribe will have the final say in all matters.

The new schema should be designed with an increased margin of safety like structures for seismic areas—there is no human community without internal conflicts. Each misunderstood or misinterpreted failure in the operation of the new version of the System will easily provoke an explosion. Confused participants will, out of habit, find a leader who will quickly offer their exclusive version of the good/bad division, adjusted for personal grievances and ambitions. Now, let's think about whether it's worth sending over armed bearers of progress right now.

Without a System built on simple and clear principles, we all lose out to our fears, insecurities, and doubts—our own "in-house" demons. The devils win, not least because the same people play on their side. These characters are enhanced by modern tools for processing and delivery of information and do everything so that we take them for granted, "as it should be." They are sure that their manipulations and attempts to use our weaknesses lead us all to the common good, and we ourselves believe in it. Except games with devils always turn out bad in the end.

Why not start like this? I'm not obligated to love a person I don't know and will treat another neutrally until they give me reasons to do the opposite. If we wish, we'll find an object that we see and understand equally, and we can do something useful for each other. I can't hit them over the head with a stick just because someone smart explained that it would be better for everyone.

I am not Mahatma Gandhi for sure. Are you? Inside me sits a primate, the same as everyone else. To deny this, one must be a liar or a saint. It gets its chance every time we settle for simple, ready-made answers that are so easy to believe. It doesn't matter what words or scientific concepts describe what it does if it's let out. No need to cling to words, you need to learn to recognize this primate to stop it in time. It is better to correct a logical error where we've made it, so as not to take an extra step to the cliff and not push another person from it. Each of us can believe in what we want, we just have to remember: We're pushing each other to the very edge of the abyss.

~ CHAPTER EIGHTEEN ~
GET RID OF CRUTCHES

Honestly, I started writing this text as a book on economics to share my thoughts: Why we try to do everything "right" and seemingly according to the rules, but when all's said and done, we can end up ass-backward. I tried to describe the situation as it is seen, not by a scientist or a financial analyst, but by someone like me—a statistical unit, or someone these smart people might analyze. It didn't work out to stay within the framework of reasoning about "income and expenses," because the real economy is what people do for each other, and sooner or later the conversation about the economy boils down to who the real actor is. Other than humans, here are just our own ideas or suggestions, such as national identities, states, companies, values, etc. Whatever we do, our result depends on how we set up our interaction using these tools or forms. If you're trying to solve a problem by making up rules to follow without using your head, you'll end up with a wonderful set of stupid limitations and not-so-gifted performers.

When there are two of these actors, it's hard enough. But the world's population will add a billion in less than fifteen years. For thousands of years, humanity has been consistently eliminating natural obstacles to population growth, while doing everything to ask ourselves as little as possible about our own responsibility.

Natural limits for the community of irresponsible mammals periodically make themselves felt, no matter how hard we try to forget about plain biology. The people population has grown, continuing to behave boorishly with each other and with the environment, and has once again received another dangerous "roommate"—the coronavirus COVID-19. We were once again reminded that we cannot and do not know everything, and that the "crown of creation" is, moreover, a colony of microorganisms with which it is forced to coexist, avoiding sharp conflicts.

At least this virus briefly distracted a good half of humanity from the most interesting thing: the war for their own idols and the already lost fight everyone has with themselves, described in the previous chapter.

You may know all this, but let's take the task itself and the System that should help us cope with it (if you'll recall, what else do we need this System for?). The bottleneck is the capacity of the healthcare system, which was not prepared for this scourge. First, it is necessary to provide all available assistance to those who fall ill and may die. Secondly, to avoid overload, we must slow down the spread as much as possible and reduce the intensity of our contacts as much as possible. Part of this movement and contact is economic interaction, or our way of earning a living, and there is no way to cross out this part without loss. It will be logical if the System, which introduces restrictions, understands all the consequences, and avoids vague generalities and symbolic gestures.

In Russia, the System responds to a new challenge in the best tradition—on the principle of "stop-there-go-here." On the one hand, everyone was released from work, on the other hand, they were forbidden to delay wages, reduce staff, and go bankrupt. How to do this for an enterprise that has stopped working and has neither sales nor revenue is a mystery. A list of enterprises whose work cannot be stopped is announced and a list of those that must be stopped. A huge number of organizations get stuck "somewhere in between ..."

Officially, a healthcare system exists here—modernized, efficient, and filled with cutting-edge equipment and professionals. In reality, for this System to help a person cope with an illness, the sick one must first cope with the System itself. It must either be defeated, spending time and effort, or bribed if money is available. Otherwise, the System simply may not see the patient.

Even after defeating the System, help may not be received. Development, optimization, and modernization actually led to a radical reduction in qualified medical personnel and equipped beds in hospitals. They've been partly replaced by virtual digital care for patients. Then you can get to the "doctor," who doesn't see or hear the patient—only a set of indicators or a picture on the printout, which must be "brought back to normal" by changing certain indicators with pills but ignoring the state of the organism as a whole. No, we somehow survive and find good doctors, but the System does little to help us in all this.

Perhaps more devastating is the fact that our ability to comprehend this new information lags markedly behind our ability to disseminate it. From the very beginning, when even specialists could not confidently and unambiguously state anything, fountains of "expert" conclusions, assessments, and forecasts were pouring out everywhere. In conjunction with them, generators of "urgent measures," restrictions, and prohibitions, went to work. It's possible to close restaurants, malls, and even schools almost simultaneously, and at the same time gather thousands of people for parades and celebrations, as happened in Russia in the summer of 2020, and believe that there is logic in this.

The real target of such inconsistent actions is the making of impressions that everything is under control and the System is in perfect working order. The inhabitant of the protective casing, out of their own rightness, again gives themselves over to their favorite pastime—a heated debate about who is to blame for everything and should pay for it all. Here we've received a wonderful occasion for significant and useless logical conclusions. When we were only at the very beginning of the story of COVID-19, but sentences to the European Union, globalism, and the "invisible hand of the market" have already rained down... and further down the list. Armed with the "best idea," they issue final verdicts one after another. The club of patriotic masochists sees salvation in an authoritarian "firm hand" and cites "lethal" statistics in favor of mainland China. Although everyone who still thinks and understands what a statistician is, is aware that the dynamics of total mortality and life expectancy will be truly relevant. Reasonable and responsible human behavior is more cost-effective than excessive restriction. And here, those countries that have learned to cope without a "strict daddy" with an average life expectancy of more than eighty years will maintain a decent handicap.

Before the coronavirus, we all had about a hundred good causes to die early. To these hundred good reasons, another one was added. Now, following the general trends, the System throws half of the available resources to a new danger, although no one has tended to all the reasons for early death that we knew before. Lack of equipment can still be made up for in a relatively short time—it can be, if not made, then bought. You can build prefabricated panel houses, set up beds there, bring in equipment, and call this decoration a medical center. With a human resource, this will not work—if there are not enough professionals, then they cannot materialize out of nowhere in two to three weeks.

And again, back to the very beginning, to understandable rules that help to separate the true from the false. In the 21st century, there's a common procedure for everyone around the world to help determine the safety and effectiveness of any vaccine or drug. It includes the third stage of clinical trials—the most massive, longest, and most costly. But in the case of Russia, here is another way to be the first to reach the finish line—halve the distance, string the ribbon yourself, cut it yourself, hire an orchestra, and celebrate the victory. And so, we do—we announce that our vaccine is ready, replacing the third stage with the simple trick of bureaucratic registration. Representatives of the System, including the most important, are carefully choosing clever words, convincing us and themselves, making tens of thousands of the first recipients of the "registered" experimental vaccine. The System will again see exactly what it wants to see and will declare its point of view to be true.

When people in a plane caught in turbulence are asked to stay in their seats and fasten their seatbelts, no one rises to fight for their rights. Everyone assumes that the crew knows what to do and understands that this lack of freedom is a necessary response to certain circumstances. It is necessary to fly through the zone of turbulence, and then it will be possible to unfasten, leaving the unfreedom behind along with the solved problem. Principled fans of control and order, along with those who suffer from a clinical need to fight and protest, will never leave the zone of turbulence. They will always find a new occasion for self-expression and noisy performances.

We can switch from military simulations to simulations of infection control, and we can invest more in medical research, in other electronic gadgets, and in building the necessary supplies. We just need to decide what is of greater value to us: a cellar of gold bars in a treasury, an arsenal stuffed to capacity, or a supply of medications and protective equipment. All these things are of economic value. People still need to find what they can do for each other without adding to the size of the dump filled with evidence of our "bounded rationality."

The brightest, most thoughtful, and useless thesis is that "the world will not be the same ...". Habits and preferences will have to be adjusted, but the world will remain where it was, along with almost eight billion inconsistent creatures.

If nothing is changed, then the same 147 million will remain in this country with the same problems, plus one more. These 147 million will still be busy arguing with each other, absorbed in their own fears and doubts, looking for the most correct ready-made answers—anything but finding solutions.

Once, "off the record," during a struggle with legislators for my hopeless strength of materials theory, I asked my interlocutor, who definitely knew how to use their brain: "You understand everything very well: Both how this problem should be solved, and how we're trying to get around this solution with the help of tricks and lies. Why are you involved in this, with those who make you deviate from the obvious over and over again?"

"How do you not understand? It's the System!" he said and went bug-eyed.

The System can be discussed until you're blue in the face, until you hiccup. You can argue, yell, be rude, make jokes, and spew forth metaphors. You can compare this System with another System, choose which one is better, add definitions, and talk about how bad it is or, conversely, how good it is. Dodge the scalding response as long as possible.

There is no System.

Why is it that every time I am told about a certain System that thinks instead of us, I see a person in front of me? Sometimes they try to hide their confusion. Sometimes it's just an asshole who wants to give themselves importance. Attempts to discern and understand the System lead nowhere, but every time I see this human being, everything falls into place.

There is a person, and there are "other" people. Look around. Do you see other real actors but humans? There is still a lot of what is proven or invented by these same people. On the one hand, these are logical rules; on the other, conventions or inventions are repeated so often and explained in such detail that they are taken for granted. Then, a phantom appears—that System behind which you can hide (I was told, "This is how it should be," I did it, and therefore everything will be fine for me). Everyone is okay with that cheap truth, which calms, helps one to become satisfied with oneself, the one that does not prick, does not make one search, and think. A person will expect salvation or protection from a ghost and will be deceived—you should not rely on your own fiction. A person will start fighting against the System and still lose because they're dealing with their own nightmare.

There is a habit of using these truths as crutches, believing that they are so right, so safe, and that without them we cannot walk. Yes, it's impossible to completely predict or model a person's behavior, but there are a number of correctly posed questions that they can and must answer themselves, taking a few steps of their own without third-party support, without crutches.

We live in a reality where our self-created phantoms and pet demons fed by our fears take up more space than living people. We pass on this reality to our children, and it will be even more difficult for them to find those solutions, those keys to the doors that we couldn't find.

There has to be a System, only it cannot be an abstraction or a chimera—it must be a schema of interaction built by people for themselves. This is our common skeleton. We need a System, in the first place, to figure out how to harm each other as little as possible, and, later, to determine how to extract the maximum benefit from our interactions. If you look at what we do, what we wear, what we eat, and what we use, every day and check labels on things around us, then you see that most of us interact according to this schema with almost half of the planet. It will deceive me in the same way that I try to deceive it, because it connects me with other people—just like me. It doesn't promise anything—it only sets algorithms for solving common problems.

I suggest that our main issue is the fact that we have a population of more than 8 billion and just one planet for all of us. It's better to put aside all the reasons for useless rhetoric about the actual version of the common truth and start with practice issues. For example, as France and Germany did in the middle of the 20th century. They fought for control over Alsace and Lorraine for centuries, but a real victory happened when both sides ceased to define who was a winner or the guilty one—they agreed on how to use disputed resources and produce coal and steel together and created a basis for the future European Union. We can argue endlessly about the non-even economic effects or the oversized bureaucracy of the EU, but for people who are living and working within a common economic space, it's hard to find a reason for a full-scale fight.

The schema that we try to construct is based on correctly posed questions that have the same interpretation and one correct answer for everyone. The questions are tough, they can be uncomfortable, and the worst part is that they suggest a clear, unambiguous answer—both to others and to yourself. It could be a better ground than all those hundred brilliant ideas that make everybody excited, but lead to thousands of various interpretations by the next step.

In short, if you don't want to be lied to further, then try to deceive yourself less often.

I see the last step here, and it is the trickiest part of the path.

~ CHAPTER NINETEEN ~
LAST STEP

Well, that's that. I've gone beyond recall—I started with platitudes and ended with notation.

The problem is—when we wipe out our own fictions from the scheme then we ought to address all uncomfortable questions to ourselves instead of addressing them to some third party like we did thousands of years ago—to an idol of a mighty spirit or some abstract general concept, to some charismatic performer who occupies the top position in a power hierarchy or to a computer's algorithm.

The right question means another step to a solution for what we are looking for. The trick is that any one of us faces such questions and ought to give an answer based on our own knowledge. It can be a choice that we make when we do not see another human, the same as we are, behind a set of clichés. It can be a small job that we replaced with an appropriate fake instead of making it as you have learned. It can be a choice between the easy way out when you just succumb to surrounding conditions and alternatives that you ought to make on your own. Right questions work like Occam's razor, leaving you nothing but a "yes" or "no" choice; it leaves no space for useless rhetoric about general rightness and helps to see the actual value of both options.

It's not a problem to face the challenge of being a part of something bigger and hiding under artificial identities. What to do when you are alone, when people around just wait when you accept the same ready-made answer and would not break an illusion of confidence and harmony? You are under pressure as far as you take a clear stand based on your own logic, you accumulate responsibility, which others prefer to avoid. It works like a simple mechanic: the most rigid part always accumulates extra loads, and your choice means you take such an uncomfortable position.

Do not ask me – how does the right question sound to you? I am not a bloody guru. I have shown my vision and how I have come to these conclusions. I have not extracted them from others' books, but learned from my own lessons and paid the full price for my own mistakes. Let me share with you a story about how to remain logical under serious pressure to succumb to group thinking.

Just imagine, you wake up in the morning and you're again tormented by the same problem: Why have I been deceived again yesterday? Trying to put something together from experience and clues to new hope, in order to move forward at least a little.

You leave the rented apartment, go down the stairs, and hear the front door slamming. Three strangers rise to meet you, talking about something of their own. You step aside and pass by without turning your head or understanding a single word.

The ground is slipping from under your feet. The sharp movement that you feel with your back makes you duck, and the first blow falls on your shoulder instead of the back of your head. Three bodies fall on you at once. Hands from all sides beat and grab at you, trying to shut your mouth. You hear, no, you feel a strangled "quiet, creep ..." and start yelling, "NO!"

They run down, they hang onto your shoulders, trying to stop you. A ball of bodies flies over the landing, rolls down the stairs, and gets stuck at the exit door. They drag you back into the entrance and press you back against the wall at the beginning of the first flight of stairs. On the right-hand side—a big man, hanging from the height of the first two steps. Another one, with a round face, opposite. He sniffles and tries to press even harder against the wall. On the left is a man with the ripest smell. He has a gun, he hit first. Now he's either pointing the barrel at your face or trying to hit you with the butt. They are NOT killing you... What do they want?

GET INTO THE HOUSE!

Here it is! Their real object is a decent amount, which you took from your partner just a night ago. Ha! Easy logic puzzle—"The two of us knew the secret, but someone betrayed us ..." Then they need this gun to scare you, not to kill. You can let them in and give them money, but you have one problem. It is a girl who is sleeping in your apartment right now. You have been dating her just for a few months and here are enough weighty, sufficient arguments so as not to be an idiot. And then everything can be explained.

To whom? Her or himself? NO!

You will agree and open... no, not the door, you will open the wormhole. Everything that you thought about yourself until now will fall into it, and everything that you will think about yourself afterward will be drawn into this chasm. You can never close it. You see how this hole opens up, and it scares you as much as the barrel of the pistol.

NO!

You don't have any "after" or "maybe." You can't do anything...pressed against the wall, you just jerk your head, and the blow is smeared and does not muffle, it just peels off the skin. Another more...warmth fills your cheek and neck. Blood. No more breath left, the image floats. They beat you and will beat you more. If all you can do is shake your head, how many seconds, how many blows do you have left, how many more hits can you take? Maybe it's time to fall?

NO!

Did you say or think that? WHY?! You can't do anything, your "no" doesn't mean anything...only the seconds that run by while you're standing on your feet have meaning—simply because you can still stand. The drums go astray. A delay. It seems they didn't have those seconds in their plan.

"TIE HIM UP!"

A fake sound, one dropped note, and you hear it. Round-faced takes out a length of white cord from somewhere in his stomach. Will he tie me up with THIS? Why does he need so much? Will it cocoon like a caterpillar? The Big Guy on top leans even harder, and tries to twist your right hand behind your back, but does it stupidly, leaving your palm free and bringing it close to his...

BALLS!

Without thinking for a second, you grab onto them, squeezing with all your might. The Big Guy grunts and bends down, opening a gap between himself and the railing. You dive in there and fight like a fish, squeezed from all sides. The railing doesn't allow Roun-faced to intervene, the Ripe Guy stays behind, you pull your left arm free of him, kick, twisting out of the vice...

That first free breath, huge as a balloon! You turn around on the first-floor landing. They're all below, like one predatory organism. Three pairs of metal eyes are looking at you...

PAUSE...

No, a vacuum in which there is simply no sound. You're waiting and sickeningly afraid of a new move. But you already have as many as eight flights of stairs behind you. In someone else's plan, they certainly were not. Ripe Guy raises the gun. You see the question in his button eyes, you feel the seconds running, but now they're running away from him... Time has stopped and stretches like a string, ready to break and cut you in half...

The three figures from the nightmare dissolve, the door slams... Exhale and the earth falls out from under your feet. The diaphragm is convulsed. You try and fail to vomit out these alien tastes and smells: the predator that thought you were food, the hand that is covering your mouth, your own animal fear. You watch as blood drips from your nose onto the tiles. On all fours, with a trouser leg torn off and teeth marks on your back, you come home...

That happened to me on January 4, 1995. I usually lose when things turn to physical violence. What I do much better is restore my self-image by explaining that it was not my failure or cowardice. Seems I am a poor fighter, but those guys gave me two good lessons.

First, I realized where my limit is, the boundary beyond which I cannot fool myself anymore. Behind this line, my lie definitely corrupts me and destroys my future. Probably, I used the stupidest way possible to gain such knowledge, but it helps if I feel such "rock bottom" under my feet when all things go bad.

Second, when I deal with another human being, it is helpful to recognize the difference between what they show me and what they actually have in mind. Do they do what is declared or just intend to impose their scenario as the only one possible? A power or a number of opponents makes sense, of course. They can put pressure on you and dominate for a while, but they are not able to switch off your brain. You can be helpless, but even your resistance for another several seconds can change a lot. Keep thinking and do not forget—they are just other human beings.

I try to find something more than a compilation of other people's thoughts and words. Then I will get a chance to establish communication with another person, who looks for answers to the same questions, and who may understand it the same way as I do. We focus on an issue that we can understand in the same way and avoid such a waste of time as any dispute where both parties see and hear nothing but their own absolute rightness. We can leave aside for a while our prejudices, find some particular common ground, and bring something meaningful to each other. Because both of us are nothing but human beings.

I know two more things for sure. There is nothing for free, and I do not believe in any real achievement without effort. It's enough to relax a little, take the easy way for a few extra times, and not be surprised if you are nullified again. When you make your own choice, when you are ready to prove and argue for that, then you get a chance to make a promise to somebody as well as to yourself. Sorry, I doubt if it works any other way.

Don't believe me?

I don't want you to believe me. I'm suggesting we think together.

Do we really have any better choice?

ABOUT THE AUTHOR

Dmitry Eremenko began his career in 1981 as a computer engineer for the Soviet army, working as part of the state-controlled economic system. When that system collapsed in 1992, he went into business for himself and has run many successful companies ever since, including fifteen years as head of the Russian branch of HOBAS, an international supplier of FRP (fiberglass reinforced plastic) pipes, and the past five years as the owner of his own business. He resides in Saint Petersburg, Russia.

www.ingramcontent.com/pod-product-compliance
Lightning Source LLC
Chambersburg PA
CBHW070142080526
44586CB00015B/1810